QUIT POINT

Adam Chamberlin & Svetoslav Matejic

QUIT POINT

UNDERSTANDING APATHY,
ENGAGEMENT, AND MOTIVATION
IN THE CLASSROOM

Quit Point
© 2018 by Times 10 Publications

These books are available at special discounts when purchased in quantity for use as premiums, promotions, fundraising, and educational use. For inquiries and details, contact us at www.Times10Books.com

Published by Times 10
Highland Heights, OH
Times10Books.com

Cover Design by Najdan Mancic
Interior Design by Steven Plummer
Editing by Carrie White-Parrish
Proofreading by Jennifer Jas

Library of Congress Cataloging-in-Publication Data is available.
ISBN: 978-1-948212-07-6
First Printing: July, 2018

TABLE OF CONTENTS

Part I: Understanding Quit Point

Recognize behavior that indicates different types of quitting

Understand the catalysts and obstacles that impact quitting

*Develop a mindset that limits quitting by emphasizing
practice, growth, collaboration, and student ownership*

Part II: Using Quit Point Strategies

*Prevent quitting through better planning and resource
design*

*Improve formative assessment and feedback through
attainable goals*

Incorporate teams, leaders, and games to prevent quitting

INTRODUCTION

ASK A DIFFERENT QUESTION

*"If you don't like the answer,
ask a different question."*

−ANONYMOUS

T WAS **4** a.m. on a warm July morning, and while most people were sleeping, one of our colleagues was frantically and repeatedly refreshing her internet page. Summer is supposed to be the time when teachers get to relax and be with their families. At least that's what most people outside the profession assume. This is not, however, always the case. Some teachers try to plan for the upcoming school year, while others can't stop thinking about the previous one. This teacher couldn't wait to get the results from her students' AP test. Every snow day, shortened bell schedule, and sick day ran through her head, and she feared for the worst. Then she thought of the high test scores and well-attended optional study session, and they revived her hopes. These scores would become her guiding focus for the next school year—evidence of her mistakes, and proof of her effort.

No wonder she couldn't sleep. The list of scores on the computer screen would indicate her success—or failure—as a teacher.

Teachers learn to define success through the achievements of their students. Relying on others isn't easy because students learn at different rates and in different ways based on their individual talents and interests. These factors are considered when teachers are planning lessons, but some students will still demonstrate little to no learning at the end of the day. Teachers tend to be a hard-working and resilient group, so they try to reach every student in the classroom—even the ones who are a daily challenge. But hard work and persistence aren't always enough. Eventually, teachers start to wonder if their students are a more significant challenge than the lesson planning. They begin to question why their students aren't working *harder*.

This question became our focus during the 2013–2014

school year, when we started to ask how we could reach more students more effectively. We believed technology could inspire students to show more engagement and effort in the classroom, so we pushed to be part of a pilot program using Chromebooks. We believed that the possibilities of a 1-to-1 classroom would allow us to embrace 21st-century learning skills and tools. Perhaps we could even leave the obstacles of traditional teaching behind. Our students would have the limitless resources of the internet at their beck and call, and we hoped that would excite them more than a textbook could. We hoped, in fact, that our experience would look more like the magical videos we'd seen in professional development sessions, where every student showed the engagement and maturity of a college student.

We knew the change to 1-to-1 would include challenges, and that we would have to be open to the kinks that would inevitably pop up in a digital classroom. But we kept a positive attitude through those challenges because the opportunities for collaboration and engagement allowed students to take more ownership of their learning. We reassured students who complained because they wanted the passive environment they had grown accustomed to, and encouraged the students who were excited to be part of a technology-driven class. No longer did students need to borrow pencils or worry about losing their papers. Our technological classroom was a breath of fresh air for students who were tired of walking into a room and listening to an adult talk—and we hoped it would change everything.

Despite our hopes and good intentions, though, it soon became clear that merely switching to a technological classroom wasn't enough to achieve the momentous change we had anticipated. Daily learning looked different, but learning outcomes still lagged.

Call it naiveté or ignorance, but we were caught off guard by the number of students that continued to give lackadaisical effort during class. Student engagement increased, particularly from the highest-achieving students, but two months into our experiment, we were still seeing the same frustrating results for our lowest-skilled students. We'd made a monumental change ... and it hadn't made any difference.

Discouraged by their lack of engagement, we decided to make additional changes. Our digital classroom provided better resources and more personalized instruction, but something was missing. Many students needed an extra push. We sought and received advice ranging from, "You have to motivate the students to work harder" to "Make the lessons more engaging and the students will care more." The first approach passed the blame onto the students, while the latter shifted the blame onto *us*, implying that we were not already doing everything possible to engage students.

And then we had an epiphany. We realized that our focus had been so set on the resources, technology, and new instructional strategies that we had neglected to consider motivation. But instead of classic carrot-and-stick approaches to motivation, like our colleagues suggested, we began to explore the difference between the more motivated and less motivated students. How did our pupils become one or the other?

Next, we fell back on a tried-and-true concept: What should we do when we don't like the answers given to a question? Ask a different question! The new goal was not simply to motivate students, but to answer the question, "What makes students quit?" Our new approach unlocked possibilities that we had never considered in the classroom. Many teachers discuss motivation and effort when they're out of solutions to long-term problems, and when they themselves begin to lose motivation. But we realized that focusing on the challenges of student apathy and motivation didn't have to be the final step before giving up on our goals. Studying the moment when every student chooses to either quit *or* continue productive effort, which we call the Quit Point, could help us find new ways to address apathy and motivation in the classroom. This was our new beginning.

Everything we learned from then on started by looking at that Quit Point.

Now, Quit Point has become the driving force for how we view, analyze, and interpret engagement in our classroom. Accounting for Quit Point provides the tools we need to better understand the challenges and solutions related to motivation. We find that many teachers look at student effort and motivation as constant elements—part of what makes up an individual student, like hair color, blood type, or dominant writing hand. But a closer examination of how people work shows a much greater range of motivation and effort than many of us realize. For example, consider how your motivation and effort vary when you read a book. Maybe the book starts slowly, so you read in smaller chunks or with limited enthusiasm while you wait for the exciting part to begin. At other times you can't put the book down, and stay up late to finish an extra chapter, putting more effort into reading than you did when you started the book. Every task we complete works the same way, with peaks and valleys of effort and motivation. Looking for those peaks and valleys is a fundamental step in incorporating Quit Point methodology.

Awareness of student Quit Points is only the first step in affecting student motivation and effort. Exploring their interests, goals, and skills gives the teacher a basis for preparing the best and most efficient ways to teach them. Embedding goals and activities in those practices allows students to take even more ownership over their work. We all have moments when it's hard to avoid procrastinating, or we know we could put in better effort or more focus. These may be professional responsibilities like grading student work in a timely manner, or household duties like mowing the lawn. Effort isn't simply a faucet we can turn on and off whenever we want. Lots of factors can make it easier or harder to be at our best.

Seeing productive effort as a process and a product of healthy habits, instead of something to be turned on or off, helps establish a mindset in which quitting isn't a default decision. Quit Points are responses to those situations when people cannot maintain their effort and experience a sudden decrease in focus and energy.

Understanding Quit Point also provides opportunities to motivate and engage low-motivation, high-quit students. High-quit students are more likely to withdraw than to attempt to overcome an obstacle. They often have a significantly different mindset about work, and much lower confidence in positive outcomes than their teachers. This often means that the concepts that motivate us as educators, such as believing we can "fail forward" and trusting initiative and effort to overcome obstacles, have a negative effect on the high-quit student. They often see our belief in students and ourselves as a trick and become even less confident in their abilities to succeed. If you are not an experienced runner, the idea of running a marathon because "you can do it" will give you a similar feeling to what low-optimism, high-quit students feel when we use ineffective motivational strategies. Just as a hot, humid day can make it harder to put effort into mowing the lawn, or the constant PA notifications at an airport can make it hard to focus on reading, the wrong motivational approach will make it harder for anyone to "turn on the faucet" and sustain focus and effort on a task.

Once we understood the lessons we learned from students quitting, we were able to discover strategies we could use to manage, delay, and avoid that point of quitting. This book collects many of the lessons and strategies we learned through our exploration of Quit Point and attempts to provide readers with ideas to immediately apply in their classrooms. We've broadly organized the strategies around concepts that increase student task value and optimism, and we've provided readers with examples that will encourage students to sustain a higher level of effort and engagement as part of their daily practice. Our goal is to help all educators immediately apply the lessons we've learned through our study of Quit Point, to make a significant, positive impact on student effort and motivation.

One final thought for this introduction: We wrote this to improve our approach to learning for all students, so they may find success in a real world that is ever-evolving. Our understanding of human psychology continues to change, while our access to data provides amazing opportunities for analyzing social interactions such as learning. The simple answers of the past are not necessarily complex enough to address the needs of 21st-century learners. We often hear our colleagues tell students what awaits them in high school, college, or the workforce, but the reality is that we try to prepare our students to succeed in a world that is changing every day in terms of technology, and we can't possibly foresee all of the needs and challenges in their futures.

Instead of teaching them to meet set goals, we must teach them to overcome all challenges, and refuse to quit.

While presenting at a technology conference, we shared this extraordinary quote from science fiction writer Arthur C. Clarke. It is both beautifully haunting and passionately optimistic at the same time. "Trying to predict the future is a discouraging and hazardous occupation. If by some miracle a prophet could describe the future exactly as it was going to take place, his predictions would sound so absurd that everybody would laugh him to scorn. The only thing we can be sure of about the future is that it will be absolutely fantastic." If we want to prepare our students for the future, we can't expect our classes to look like the schools of the past, or use education strategies of old, but should instead be ready to embrace anything, including the absurd and absolutely fantastic. It is our hope that the concepts included in this book are a key to unlocking just that.

PART I

UNDERSTANDING QUIT POINT

CHAPTER 1

WHAT IS QUIT POINT AND HOW DOES IT IMPACT STUDENTS?

Recognize behavior that indicates different types of quitting

"Winners quit all the time. They just quit the right stuff at the right time."

—SETH GODIN

WE ALL SPEND a lot of time praising traits like hard work, determination, perseverance, and grit—and noting their importance in overcoming any challenge or obstacle. Whether in the classroom, office, or on the athletic field, we know these are the elements of achievement and success. In fact, these traits are so deeply embedded in our culture that one of the clearest paths to winning an Oscar for best picture is to highlight a story of people (or sometimes Hobbits) overcoming obstacles. Films such as *Titanic, The Lord of the Rings, Gladiator, The King's Speech,* and *12 Years A Slave* won awards by celebrating those who overcame adversity. And our appreciation for determination and resilience isn't limited to the big screen.

Runners proudly display "26.2" bumper stickers, showing off to the world that they completed a marathon. We celebrate champions and innovators like Michael Jordan and Thomas Edison—who overcame adversity and gained great success. What if Michael Jordan had given up after he was cut from his high school basketball team? What if Thomas Edison had given up after his hundredth attempt at a longer-lasting light bulb? Certainly, our world would be a colder, emptier place if our heroes gave up before they had a chance to inspire generations.

> We don't want our effectiveness as teachers to be defined by the moments in which we quit, so we shouldn't base our judgments of student potential on their least resilient moments.

Stories like these are so celebrated that quitting has become a dirty word. People see quitting as the end of the story, or a moment we should regret and forget. But a closer look at quitting shows that it is an important component in how we handle difficult tasks. The reality is that everyone quits—even Michael Jordan and Thomas Edison. Michael Jordan was an exceptional athlete with a skill set and determination that helped him excel in the world of professional basketball, but that didn't keep him from quitting professional baseball. Thomas Edison stuck with ideas that had potential but was willing to bail on his less interesting ideas like the electric pen.

If they hadn't quit on the things that didn't work for them, they never would have focused on what they did well. Michael Jordan would have been an average baseball player who bounced around the minor leagues for a few years, and Thomas Edison would have spent his energy running a failed cement company. If our champions can quit and still be heroes, we need to reconsider how quitting fits into *our* goals.

The point is to recognize that everyone quits, and it's not always a problem. Even teachers quit at times. They may leave a pile of papers ungraded, put off calling the parents of a challenging student, or decide a video may be a good shortcut for a lesson. We don't want our effectiveness as teachers to be defined by the moments in which we quit, so we shouldn't base our judgments of student potential on their least resilient moments. It may be hard to admit that our students, even those who struggle in the classroom, can show tremendous amounts of determination and grit—but that doesn't make it any less true.

STUDENTS TRY HARD, JUST NOT ALWAYS AT SCHOOL

Sometimes, instead of academic effort, students will focus their energy on "fairness" or helping a friend with a problem. Students will push through exhaustion to play games for an extra hour when their parents are asleep. Inevitably, the day after popular new video games are released, we see a group of students who have no energy to work hard in the classroom, because they played "just one more time" the night before. Others may show their determination by spending an extra hour making sure their hair and clothes are perfect, instead of doing their homework.

Unfortunately, many students must show resilience just to make it to school every morning. They overcome hunger, abusive situations, depression, personal struggles, illness, acting as parental figures for younger siblings, and more, before setting foot in a classroom.

Each of these variations requires recognition, because that is how we as educators come to understand why students quit differently than teachers when it comes to school. These variables play a vital role in showing the kinds of challenges people are willing to persevere through ... and the challenges that will lead to quitting. Instead of lamenting the fact that students don't work harder, teachers can structure their classes in a way that highlights *existing* student abilities. This knowledge allows educators to avoid more Quit Points and personalize instruction in ways that traditional educational frameworks have not widely considered.

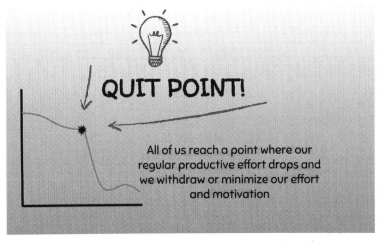

Figure 1.1: The point when individuals begin exerting less effort.

REGULAR PRODUCTIVE EFFORT

Quit Point is the moment when an individual's productive energy toward a specific goal drops, causing withdrawal or minimized effort. As people work toward accomplishing a goal (washing the dishes, learning a geometric theorem, running a marathon, etc.), they must maintain a consistent level of effort. Many people assume that level of effort is the equivalent of using 100 percent of their energy. And when the options are to work harder and give even more effort—or give up entirely—those who have already maximized their effort and have not yet overcome their challenges, simply quit.

Other times, people will divide their attention and effort among many goals and give up during a task that they should have easily completed. It is as easy to put a plate in the dishwasher as it is the sink. However, if you are at work all day, come home to take care of your kids, and are tired from your long day, the extra effort it takes to put the plate in the dishwasher may be more than you can give.

Following that same reasoning, students who struggle aren't necessarily being lazy when they fail at working just a little bit harder. Hard work is relative and variable, not a constant value. A student who comes up against challenges and obstacles might not be *able* to overcome them, no matter how hard he or she works. That doesn't mean they're lazy; just that the challenge is beyond their means.

For this reason, we focus on the concept of "Regular Productive Effort" instead of hard work. "Regular" implies a degree of consistency, and "productive" implies movement—in this case, toward the desired goal. A person can show Regular Productive Effort at mowing the lawn, but it would be absurd to think of one person mowing the lawn "harder" than another person. Consistent movement toward the goal means there is Regular Productive Effort. In the classroom, instead of trying to measure or quantify the exertion and energy students put into their learning, we can study the habits they exhibit when engaged in Regular Productive Effort, compared to those they demonstrate after reaching their Quit Point. Knowing the difference between these habits allows us to determine the moment a student reaches that Quit Point. We can also better differentiate between Regular Productive Effort and the behaviors students show when they try to hide the fact that they have quit.

SYMPTOMS OF HITTING QUIT POINT

When people hit their Quit Point, they begin to demonstrate forms of procrastination, distraction, or avoidance. They understand the importance of completing the task but are unable to focus their effort toward achieving their goal on time. Thomas Jefferson reminds us to "Never put off for tomorrow, what you can do today." While that may sound inspiring, Mark Twain's wit was much more applicable for most people when he revised Jefferson's quote to: "Never put off till tomorrow what may be done the day after tomorrow just as well."

While Twain makes light of the issue, the reality is that once a person has reached the Quit Point, it is easier to continue procrastinating than it is to increase the effort.

Distraction is possibly the most common symptom of Quit Point because students have so many non-academic priorities that compete for their time and attention. For many teachers, the cell phone is the ultimate symbol of this competition for students' attention. The amount of information and entertainment possibilities via technology is greater than ever. Instead of passing notes and throwing spitballs, students can just turn to their personal devices—and the distraction they provide. Distraction is a logical response to situations that begin to require more energy to maintain consistent productivity. Once the energy it takes to stay focused is more than a student can sustain, the only option is to lose focus. Teachers curse the invention of the cell phone because they believe it is the source of distraction, but we need to understand that those devices may not cause quitting. They may instead be a student's way of coping with having reached obstacles that led to the Quit Point.

The most obvious symptom of a student hitting the Quit Point is avoidance. When students refuse to try assignments, fail to participate, or fall asleep in class, even a bystander can see that they've given up on class goals. To the frustrated classroom teacher, staying awake in class seems like a simple and easily accomplished request. However, just like the sink full of dishes can overwhelm the most resilient adult after a day of work, this straightforward task can prove to be too much for a student who has reached a limit.

Recognizing avoidance as a symptom of Quit Point allows us to search for the variable that led to this outcome, rather than giving in to frustration. From the student's perspective, the consequences of avoidance may be less stressful than the idea of trying to sustain any effort at all.

Recognizing that these behaviors are symptoms allows educators to address the factors that cause Quit Point in the first place. To solve the problem, you must

> When a student is actively engaged in learning, the teacher will not see procrastination, distraction, or avoidance. The moment when quitting begins is when students first start to show the Quit Point habits—and shift into different stages of the continuum.

treat the underlying cause. Failure to do so will lead to the students quitting—and becoming so used to quitting that only the most intensive interventions have any hope of helping them.

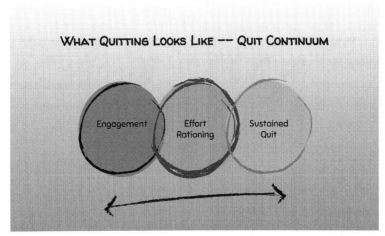

Figure 1.2: Quitting takes many forms along the continuum. Helping people shift their energy toward engagement results in greater productivity and learning over time.

THE PHASES OF QUITTING

Once educators are aware of student Quit Points, they begin to recognize effort as being on a continuum rather than an all-or-nothing concept. Engagement is the goal of the classroom because that is when the most learning occurs. Students actively participate, cooperate, and take ownership of their education. When a student is actively engaged in learning, the teacher will not see procrastination, distraction, or avoidance. The moment when quitting begins is when students first start to show the Quit Point habits—and shift into different stages of the continuum. And from that first point, they may progress all the way to quitting, and this may become their default action.

Sustained Quit is at the opposite end of the continuum from engagement. This type of quitting is easy to observe because students try to avoid any learning. Depending on the student, avoidance may take the form of sleeping in class, exhibiting disruptive behaviors, or refusing to attempt class work. Sustained Quit is the most extreme case of quitting, and the most difficult to manage. Educators must immediately recognize that a student is not going to be motivated to move from a position of Sustained Quit to one of engagement. Once students have reached that level, we need to help them shift their motivation to Effort Rationing before we can hope for active participation again.

Effort Rationing is an element of Quit Point that occurs when students feel they cannot or should not sustain a consistent, productive effort for the duration of a task. An example of Effort Rationing during reading could be skimming. Students look like they are reading but are only trying to learn enough to seem like they're paying attention. Procrastination, distraction, and avoidance still occur at this stage but are more difficult to detect because students will try to display regular work habits, even though their efforts have dropped. It is challenging for a teacher in a traditional classroom to differentiate Regular Productive Effort from Effort Rationing because of how similar they can appear. If teachers fail to recognize the difference between real and simulated work habits, it can result in less learning outcomes for students.

Nonetheless, Effort Rationing can be a positive move on the continuum for a student who previously displayed symptoms of Sustained Quitting. Full engagement might be an unrealistic expectation for students whose original plan in class was to put their heads down for a nap. An intermediate step of partial participation is a more attainable goal in these situations. For example, skimming can still result in recognizing keywords and vocabulary, and it can be a bridge to full engagement. Students exhibiting symptoms of Sustained Quit are challenging to reset or re-engage because, like athletes, they can't usually perform at their best without a warm-up. Effort Rationing can be the warm-up they need before re-engaging.

Understanding the importance of Effort Rationing on the Quit Continuum makes it easier to engage students in the learning process. Students are only one step away from fully participating, and only a Quit Point away from Sustained Quit and withdrawal. Effort Rationing is usually the default level of engagement and motivation when students walk into a classroom. They observe and evaluate how exciting, challenging, or stressful a lesson will be, and then shift their effort accordingly. Students might increase their engagement for an interesting lesson, but if they decide that the experience does not match their priorities, they might just as easily turn to Sustained Quit.

If students are in Effort Rationing mode, however, they are only a step from real engagement. Teachers can redirect these students more easily because they maintain at least a minimal effort toward class goals. For example, the student who is skimming through a reading assignment is not fully engaged in the reading but is doing something more productive than not reading at all. It would be easier to move a student from skimming to real reading than it would be to help a sleeping student suddenly engage with the class reading. Most teachers, however, focus on students in Sustained Quit and allow students in Effort Rationing to slide—which is a missed opportunity.

This tendency does not apply to students alone. Think about your last staff meeting and assess your engagement. Were you engaged with your peers in working toward a common goal? Or were you participating only enough to avoid criticism from your boss before the designated end time? If you answered with the latter, don't feel too badly. The reality is that Effort Rationing isn't always disruptive to achieving our goals—but also should not be confused with Regular Productive Effort just because it lacks clear indicators of disengagement. Fortunately, administrators do not attempt to recognize Effort Rationing during meetings. If they tried, they would not have the time or energy to accomplish any of the meeting tasks.

Knowing and being able to recognize these stops along the Quit Continuum provide us with valuable information about student learning and motivation, and give us the ability to quickly judge each student's engagement level. Even knowing what our students' personal Quit Points might be—allows us to move quickly and effectively.

Quit Point is a tool for helping students maximize their potential. The idea is that even those who fail to meet the high standards will still reach far beyond what they would have achieved under normal circumstances. This notion sounds reasonable and may even work for students who come into the classroom with the lowest risk of quitting. But what are educators to do for the multitude of students who walk into our classes with a high Quit Point risk? Will students with little optimism still strive for any target? Or will they quit after the first sign of adversity? Will they, in fact, give up before the class has even begun, because they are buried by long- and short-term obstacles, making most tasks seem out of reach?

Students who have a high Quit Point risk are likely to withdraw rather than attempt to overcome an obstacle. They often have a significantly different mindset about work than their teachers. The result is that the things that motivate us as educators don't inspire confidence in these students. Emphasizing short-term sacrifice for long-term success, and the belief that we can "fail forward," can have negative effects on high-quit students, because it sets the bar too high. They have more experience in quitting than they have determination and resilience. And since they have no history of success, they see teachers' beliefs in students as a trick—for which they are not going to fall. This, in turn, makes them even less confident.

By observing individual Quit Points, though, we can finally give students what they need. We can better understand the level of effort they're giving in the classroom, and provide them with reasonable goals that fit their paths, rather than the one-size-fits-all mold we've been using for so long.

TEACHER TAKEAWAY

It is essential to recognize that everyone quits, including at school. As educators, it is common to expect students not to give up, because our experiences and expectations related to education helped *us* to persevere throughout formal schooling. However, many of our students quit because, based on their own experiences, it is a better choice than struggling throughout each day or even each class. These choices are not because they don't want to be successful—and yet that is how teachers often perceive students' lack of effort.

Quitting can look different for each student and can take the form of both Effort Rationing and Sustained Quitting. While most teachers can quickly identify Sustained Quitting, many struggle to accurately differentiate between Effort Rationing and Regular Productive Effort. If a classroom is teacher-centered, a student might appear to be engaged, while a closer assessment would show that the student is Effort Rationing. From there, it is a short step to Sustained Quit—and to true engagement. Recognizing student effort through the concept of Quit Point allows teachers to change their approaches in the classroom, reduce student quitting, and increase effort and engagement.

Classroom Climate and Culture	
Limited	❏ Students wait for teacher directions before focusing on classroom goals ❏ Students are reluctant to work with their peers on common learning goals ❏ Students often ignore classroom rules
Progressing	❏ Students come to the classroom and ask the teacher about how they should start the day ❏ Students will collaborate with their peers toward common goals when prompted by the teacher ❏ Students follow classroom rules when reminded by the teacher
Advanced	❏ Students work together to begin learning as soon as they enter the classroom ❏ Students are empowered to regularly collaborate with peers and initiate discussions with the teacher about common goals ❏ Students help establish and reinforce classroom rules

Figure 1.3: Classroom Climate and Culture Rubric

Student Work Habits	
Limited	❏ Students rarely begin assignments without direct oversight from the teacher ❏ Students judge the quality of their work solely by completion ❏ Students regularly procrastinate or rush through assignments
Progressing	❏ Students regularly show productive effort toward completing their assignments ❏ Students are willing to revise and improve their work ❏ Student effort is inconsistent from day to day
Advanced	❏ Students are empowered to collaborate with peers to improve assignments ❏ Students ask for feedback from peers and the teacher to help demonstrate high-level understanding ❏ Students demonstrate metacognition and adapt to assignments based on needs

Figure 1.4: Student Work Habits Rubric

Instructional Strategies	
Limited	❑ Students rarely have the opportunity to demonstrate active learning ❑ Student learning is expected to be demonstrated on the teacher's schedule ❑ Students are assigned similar assignments every year
Progressing	❑ Students sometimes have the opportunity to demonstrate active learning ❑ Students have some independent time when learning ❑ Student assignments or assessments are modified based on learning needs
Advanced	❑ Students frequently have the opportunity to demonstrate active learning ❑ Students have the flexibility to learn at their own pace ❑ Students' learning expectations are differentiated based on individual needs and with the support of other teachers

Figure 1.5: Instructional Strategies Rubric

Motivation and Incentives	
Limited	❑ Students only judge the importance of work based on the impact on their grade ❑ Students only work to avoid negative consequences ❑ Students try to complete work early in order to focus on non-academic interests
Progressing	❑ Students judge their work based on the classroom expectations of high-quality work ❑ Students are confident achievement will be recognized ❑ Student personal interests are incorporated in learning goals and classroom rewards
Advanced	❑ Students judge their work based on high classroom expectations and how well they meet their personal goals ❑ Student achievements are respected by peers and the teacher ❑ Students choose to use time outside of class to reach and support personal and peer goals

Figure 1.6: Motivation and Incentives Rubric

CHAPTER 2

VARIABLES THAT INFLUENCE QUIT POINT

Understand the catalysts and obstacles that impact quitting

"Do something. If it works, do more of it. If it doesn't, do something else."
—FRANKLIN D. ROOSEVELT

NOW THAT WE understand what Quit Point is—and how it can help us as teachers—it's important to understand how it happens. Part of our research was to understand why our students reached a Quit Point, and when the process started. We categorized these starting variables as broad concepts: obstacles that diverted an individual's effort, and catalysts that focused an individual's energy. In the classroom, these obstacles led away from engagement and toward a Quit Point, while catalysts led to better engagement during learning activities.

Most important, we found that the variables could shift from day to day, or even at different points throughout a lesson.

Long-term variables, for example, often have the most significant impact on a student's average output over prolonged periods of time. These variables are well established before students reach the classroom and come from experiences connected to their family backgrounds. Sometimes these issues can be minor, such as a need for attention. Other times, such as in a home that has substance abuse problems, these variables might have to do with emotional and physical safety. Students who have issues like that for an extended period are more likely to fall behind, because they need to devote more energy to their basic needs and stability than students from healthy homes. These students, through no fault of their own, will dedicate less productive effort toward learning than students who experience more positive long-term variables.

Students who have a healthy support system and coping skills, as well as socioemotional stability, will exhibit more resilience in the face of everyday challenges, and will hit their

Quit Points later. If their home environment provides for their primary needs, school becomes a place where they can devote more energy toward learning. A supportive family environment outside of school helps nurture the catalysts of optimism, task value, and resiliency—and makes quitting less likely. On the other hand, students with significant family issues are more likely to quit in the face of adversity.

Understanding these variables is essential to understanding a student's risk of quitting. Knowing how long a student has been dealing with the variables is just as important, because long-term issues are more difficult to resolve quickly.

> When students face challenges to learning, an optimistic outlook encourages them to persevere. Students who are pessimistic about their goals, however, are more likely to quit.

Teachers should also consider variables that impact student effort in the short-term. Short-term factors usually occur unexpectedly, but can still have a powerful impact on student Quit Points. An argument with a friend on the way to school can increase the chance of quitting for the entire school day. The frustration from those brief moments on the bus may carry over to the classroom and reduce a student's ability to maintain Regular Productive Effort. An eagerly anticipated field trip, however, can be the catalyst for a student's enthusiasm about learning. The optimism of having a good day in school because of the field trip may only be temporary, but it can make a significant impact on the student's effort, including on tasks not connected to the field trip.

Optimism is often the critical variable in overcoming short- and long-term obstacles. Even students with all the prerequisite skills and background for success will struggle to avoid quitting when they confront a task that decreases their optimism. When students face challenges to learning, an optimistic outlook encourages them to persevere. Students who are pessimistic about their goals, however, are more likely to quit. For this reason, habitual quitters can sometimes outperform high achievers—if they are having a day when they have more optimism than the "better" students. A frequent quitter whose only goal is to complete an assignment with Effort Rationing may be optimistic about accomplishing that task, and therefore find success. Meanwhile, the student who routinely achieves at a high level may be less optimistic, because that student's goal is to continue the success, not just complete the assignment.

The irony of this scenario is that honor roll students may quit well before their peers if they believe they're at risk for earning a poor grade. Their perceived outcome does not align with their definition of success, and they lose their optimism—and their motivation for continuing. Lower-achieving students can be highly optimistic because they are confident in their ability to earn a D. Understanding how variables such as optimism create catalysts and increase student effort allows teachers to better recognize—and limit—the impact of Quit Point in the classroom.

In this chapter, we break down the variables that impact a student Quit Point: optimism, task value, resilience, long-term obstacles, and short-term obstacles. The "equation" that we created (Figure 2.1) is not designed for plugging in quantities for a result. Instead, it serves as a visual representation of how we categorize variables that impact effort. The variables above the line have a positive impact on student effort and serve as catalysts that decrease the likelihood of a Quit Point. For example, the more optimistic a student is about a successful outcome, the more likely the student is to persist through challenges with regular effort and avoid a Quit Point. Conversely, the variables below the line negatively impact effort, making it more likely for a student to hit a Quit Point. The student who fought with a friend has less chance of succeeding in the challenges of the classroom because of the negative impact of that short-term obstacle.

Some factors in this equation are within our control, while others are part of the student's personality, upbringing, or living environment. Our classroom climate and learning expectations are not likely to resolve the problems associated with a student whose parents are going through a divorce. However, we can directly influence the student's level of optimism regarding the challenges of the classroom if we consider all of the variables, and act accordingly. No classroom teacher can single-handedly address all the variables related to Quit Point. Instead, we use the equation to focus on aspects that we *can* influence.

$$\text{EFFORT} = \frac{\text{OPTIMISM} \times \text{TASK VALUE} \times \text{RESILIENCE}}{\text{LONG TERM OBSTACLES} \times \text{SHORT TERM OBSTACLES}}$$

QUIT POINT EQUATION

How we break down the elements that make a Quit Point more or less likely

Figure 2.1: Using strategies to increase the variables on the top and decrease the variables on the bottom will help students achieve higher levels of effort.

OPTIMISM

Optimism is a factor that teachers can directly influence when addressing Quit Points. We focus on short-term, immediate optimism as it relates to students' perceptions of their responsibilities in the classroom. Students' first few minutes in class or on an assignment can determine their confidence for the rest of the lesson. Teachers focus on other factors, such as grit and resilience, instead of optimism, because they believe optimism is a character trait that simply runs in opposition to pessimism. You may view yourself as optimistic vs. pessimistic, or as a glass-half-empty vs. glass-half-full person. Most people do. A brief look at the research on optimism, however, will help illustrate how we can influence student optimism to achieve our goal of avoiding Quit Points.

Dr. Martin Seligman's research on optimism resulted in his theory of Learned Helplessness. His research involved dogs that were subjected to electrical shocks, and the results led to the development of this theory. One group of dogs was taught to stop the shock by using a lever. The other group of dogs had no control over the outcome. Even when yoked with dogs who could turn off the shock, the second group of dogs did not attempt to avoid the discomfort. These dogs had reached their Quit Point and accepted the pain as inevitable.

The second part of the study placed the dogs in a shuttle box with a low partition. When one side of the box was shocked, the dogs could jump over the barrier. What was alarming about this part of the study was that many of the dogs who were conditioned to believe they had no control would not try to escape the shock by jumping to the other side, as the rest of the dogs did. Instead, some of those dogs passively gave up and accepted the outcome. They had been taught to believe they had no control over their situation, and so they quit.

When we first came across this study while researching Quit Point, we immediately compared it to what we had seen in the classroom. Every year, we had a handful of students who approached the final exam needing to pass it to receive credit for the entire course. From a teacher's point of view, this seems like a simple problem to solve. Students could avoid failing a class or potentially failing to graduate by merely engaging in review work and focusing on the exam. Teachers encouraged these students to forget past failures and focus their efforts on passing the exam. Some students used this encouragement to work harder and ensure a passing grade—but others seemed resigned to failure.

The conclusion was simple: Our approach wasn't addressing the underlying cause of why this second group of students had quit.

What often happens with these students who are accustomed to reaching their Quit Point is like what Seligman saw in his experiments. Students who do not feel like they are in control of their academic success are likely to quit. Those who make a habit of giving up accept a lower standard of achievement due to their lack of optimism about learning. Students may not need to struggle or work particularly hard to prepare for an exam; completing their review work should be enough for most students to pass. But that might not be enough to motivate them—just as an opportunistic dog wasn't enough of a catalyst to motivate dogs that had learned to accept a painful shock. The teacher optimistically presents the task of the exam to students, only to be frustrated when students respond pessimistically and fail to prepare at all.

Students don't always share our optimism when it comes to situations in which schoolwork is the solution to their challenges. Most teachers trust that effort in the classroom leads to success, because that was their personal experience. At-risk students are more likely to be disappointed with the results of their efforts, however, because they don't match the teacher's expectations. This lack of optimism is why presenting a student with a "simple task" that requires "a little effort" can cause the student to lose confidence and feel helpless. The variable that the teacher sees as the solution—effort—is the same variable that the student understands as the cause of the disappointment. Seligman compares the momentary helplessness of dealing with that contradiction to a punch in the stomach.

Optimism research describes three distinct ways in which people respond to situations. These responses will significantly influence their level of optimism. These are:

- Permanence
- Pervasiveness
- Personalization

Permanence refers to the timeline by which students view a certain obstacle. When they are addressing a condition, do they view it as permanent, as in "I'm not good at math," or temporary, as in "I'm struggling with fractions"? Teachers can build optimism in their students by reinforcing the temporary nature of setbacks. Students who understand that their struggle with fractions is brief will be less likely to reach a Quit Point in math class. Reinforcing more permanent positive traits can also build optimism. Some students have strong collaborative learning skills, so assigning work that allows them to use these skills will cause them to be more optimistic than if teachers expect them to work independently.

Pervasiveness refers to how much students allow obstacles to reach from one section of their lives into another. When faced with obstacles, some people can compartmentalize the problem, preventing it from spilling into other parts of their lives. One person can view a morning commute full of traffic delays as just that, causing stress on the drive but not impacting other parts of the day. Others can allow it to frame the entire workday. People will affect their own optimism for the day with how pervasive they allow a problem to be. For example, when a student does not get along with a teacher, is the student able to be specific with the explanation, as in "Mr. Chamberlin singles me out in class," or does the student apply a broad pervasiveness to the situation, as in "Teachers always blame me for everything"? Teachers can build student optimism by stressing the unique nature of challenges and encouraging students to compartmentalize problems. They can contain obstacles so they have less influence on students wanting to quit.

> As teachers, we can influence a student's optimism by controlling the situation. We can attempt to reduce the likelihood of student Quit Points by focusing on optimism and reasonable, short-term outcomes.

Personalization is the habit of controlling obstacles. Some people personalize events by focusing on the impact their actions have on their success. They feel a great deal of control over outcomes. Those who lack this trait will view results as being controlled by other people's actions. For instance, when students do well, they can attribute the outcome to the hard work they put into the task, or to the fact that the teacher decided to give an easy assignment. Students who do not feel in control of their learning are more likely to quit. Students facing the high-stakes final exam will not put in much effort if they don't understand that their actions (studying) are more critical to the results than the teacher's actions (the level of difficulty of the exam). If students see positive situations as merely lucky or due to someone else's actions, they will be less likely to continue to give effort. Students who understand the connections between their actions and positive outcomes will persevere through obstacles, because they believe they will see the fruit of their labor.

This means that we as teachers can influence a student's optimism by controlling the situation. We can attempt to reduce the likelihood of student Quit Points by focusing on optimism and reasonable, short-term outcomes. This strategy provides opportunities for students to learn that setbacks are temporary, and results are always under their control. They won't believe negative consequences are pervasive or permanent when they experience success on a regular basis. Short-term optimism also helps students personalize their definition of success. It takes countless actions and decisions to achieve broad goals, such as graduating on time or earning an A.

Emphasizing these smaller actions helps shift student definitions of success to more specific personal goals.

Student A	Student B
This student has been labeled since elementary school as "gifted." Their closest group of friends are also tracked in advanced courses. Expectations from their parents are that only As and Bs are acceptable. Therefore, the student defines success as achieving high grades.	This student has been tracked as a gifted learner since elementary school, but expectations from parents regarding school are to "do your best" and "work hard." While this student still strives for high grades, they are also concerned with their effort.
When faced with adversity, this student evaluates their achievement relative to the grades they earn. When this student struggles to grasp a difficult concept or new skill, they lose optimism because the "gifted" label has become part of their identity. They perceive "gifted" students as not having to give much effort. Struggling in school may cause them to quit rather than working harder than their peers.	When faced with adversity, this student is not likely to perceive the adversity as permanent. It is easy to accept effort rationing if the result is As and Bs, but this student is more likely to increase effort while challenged academically because their perception of success is not defined simply by grades.

Figure 2.2: How students define success impacts how they respond to certain situations. Thinking of success in terms of learning and growth rather than absolute measures causes individuals to process adversity differently.

TASK VALUE

The next variable in the Quit Point equation is task value. Simply put, if a student views a task as necessary, the student will show productive effort rather than quitting. As a student's task value wanes, the likelihood of reaching a Quit Point increases. When people see a task as extremely important, such as helping a toddler who fell and hit his head, they will put a lot of energy toward resolving the situation, no matter how tired they are. Staff meetings, however, are merely an obligation many educators must go through. Teachers who don't see much value in a staff meeting will Effort Ration and grade papers rather than being fully engaged in the meeting. We can use this reality to prepare a learning environment that provides greater task value, and therefore limits the risk of students quitting.

Task value—like optimism—is an individual variable. Each student attributes a value to a lesson, a specific subject matter, or even school in general. And this value is just as changeable as optimism. A clear example of just how quickly task value can change is in the amount of effort demonstrated by students when a substitute teacher is in the room. Student behaviors toward a substitute teacher are different than those when the full-time teacher is present. This difference occurs in large part because a substitute teacher's classroom activities often fall into the category of busywork. These assignments fill up the time but don't necessarily support the learning goals. Not surprisingly, students tend to value this busywork less than regular assignments, because it is not as relevant to their learning experience and goals. This perceived lack of value increases the potential for students to reach their Quit Points.

Task value can also shift based on unexpected circumstances. Just like adults, students continuously evaluate the significance of moments throughout their day. Even if a sink full of dishes has been waiting for several days, you would never say that cleaning those dirty dishes was more important than an unexpected family emergency. One can only imagine what would happen to a husband who told his pregnant wife that her contractions would have to wait until he'd put away the dishes! Situations pop up unexpectedly and can shift our task value in the short term and make us more likely to quit another activity—and this is as true in the classroom as it is anywhere else.

Teachers must recognize short-term obstacles and their impacts on task value, and how quickly they might push a student toward a Quit Point. In our modern world of constant connectivity, social media updates can derail a student's effort by shifting the short-term task value. At the moment of discovery, all other activities become less important—including the learning that would have occurred. News that comes across social media can cause students to Effort Ration or even progress to Sustained Quit, just because their task values have shifted. Even students who usually engage in the classroom can fall victim to news that is more important to them at that given moment.

Long-term factors can also impact task value. Students quit when they do not see the relevance of education to their lives outside of school. If a student does not have family members that finished high school, it is difficult for that student to apply high task value toward graduation, because they have not personally witnessed the benefits of a diploma. This long-term factor could make it difficult for the student to find value in completing daily assignments. The age-old questions of "How will this help me?" or "When will I ever use this?" are questions about task value. These questions from students are warning signs that quitting is imminent. If teachers only provide a cliché answer, many kids will see that as a sign of low task value and be more likely to quit. Educators that successfully answer the questions, though, and address the long-term factors appropriately, can make a significant impact on the level of importance their students assign to learning.

Students don't necessarily have to be pessimistic about completing school to struggle in their search for long-term task value. Many students are not yet sure what kind of life they want after graduation. Some go to college, others search for a job, and some choose to live at home while they sort out their plans. We can't expect every student to walk into a classroom and have a clear understanding of his or her college and career plans. The same student may want to be a fireman when in kindergarten, a doctor when in middle school, and a banker while in high school. These changing ambitions are why teachers need to be careful not to overemphasize the career connections of their classes. If that is the only value that a teacher can ascribe to learning, some students will shut down when the lesson doesn't seem to relate to their goals.

The good news about task value is that teachers can positively impact this as well. A more productive approach to helping students shift their motivation is to align the learning process to reflect student values. This strategy is a reversal of the teacher-defined task value described in the example above. The teacher can apply students' values and motivations to learning, instead of assigning value with grades, points, or examples of how learning will apply later in life. For example, students who enjoy competition will better understand the importance of a lesson about presidential elections if the teacher compares it to areas in which students compete. By shifting the focus onto the students' values, the teacher has a better chance of increasing task value and limiting the risk of quitting.

The research of Susan Fowler, a leading scholar, educator, and consultant on motivation, supports this approach. Her work reminds us that people's perceived lack of motivation is just a case of individuals not being motivated in the same way as the motivator. Many teachers address motivation as if they're moving unmotivated students toward productive work. In many cases, the problem is not a complete lack of motivation, but that the students are interested in non-academic topics. In that case, student motivation may not align with what the teacher values. A more productive approach, according to Fowler, is to help students shift their motivation by aligning the learning process to reflect their own values.

Just as personalization is helpful when attempting to build optimism, it can also be a useful strategy when helping students find more value in the assigned tasks in class. Teachers can't artificially increase task value by emphasizing the impact the assignment would have on grades. Grades may be relevant to many students, but school is supposed to be about learning and creating a foundation for future achievement. Being able to talk with individual students, show an understanding of their motivations, and attempt to make a connection between motivations and assigned tasks is a more powerful method of building task value than holding grades over students' heads.

RESILIENCE

Understanding why individual students show resilience in the face of obstacles is the final catalyst of our equation. When discussing this variable, we mean the characteristic that allows some people to bounce back from setbacks and grind out productive work. Some refer to it as "stick-to-itiveness," while Angela Duckworth's research on the subject popularized the term "grit." It is an ability to persevere through the tasks that do not bring the individual either task value or optimism. This character trait is on the top of the equation because nurturing more of it will cause students to give more consistent effort and quit less.

Resilience often pops up where you least expect it, and sometimes students will demonstrate surprising resistance to Quit Points. When we first introduced our classroom set of Chromebooks, we had widespread network access problems. Some students gave up the first time they encountered an obstacle. If we're honest, we also wanted to curl up like scared armadillos every time we experienced a technical mishap. Most others gave up when the directions we provided weren't enough to log in. A small group, however, tried strategies that we hadn't even considered. Those students continued to problem-solve until they found a solution—or were told to give up and move on. This last group wasn't necessarily more technologically inclined than their peers. They just had more stamina when it came to resisting the desire to quit.

So how do some students have it while others don't? Factors outside the classroom profoundly influence student resilience. One element that contributes to a student's ability to persevere is family and home life. Does the student have positive adult role models and mentors? Is the family a source of stability and support, or is it an additional stressor for the student to overcome? Having a trusted adult figure that models strong communication and problem-solving skills can play a significant role in a student's resilience. Seeing the people closest to them work through moments that cause others to quit helps students understand how to push through challenging situations. This support structure provides an outlet for dealing with obstacles and intense emotions.

Conversely, a lack of support structure from family members or adults can have a significantly adverse effect on a student's resilience.

Personal factors also contribute to a student's resilience. Learning an instrument or playing a sport requires significant amounts of perseverance and patience. People are often more passionate about these pursuits than their learning, and that passion can motivate them to work through the unavoidable obstacle of frustration that comes along with mastering high-level activities. And every time people fight through that frustration, they gain experience in dealing with obstacles. The ability to overcome challenges develops over time with the accumulation of little wins. Some students transfer the resilience of those small victories to the classroom and show more resistance to quitting.

Pursuing one's passions and hobbies isn't the only way to learn resilience. Some cases show that individuals with significant challenges, such as learning or physical disabilities, persevere and are successful precisely because they learned strategies for overcoming circumstances that would limit others. Many people have dyslexia, which causes tremendous difficulty with learning early in life. Still, a handful of the world's most successful individuals were able to overcome those sorts of educational obstacles. Richard Branson, founder of Virgin Records, and Brian Grazer, Hollywood producer, developed strategies for persevering through that disability. A steadfast resiliency that refused to let them quit made their achievements possible.

Understanding which students demonstrate higher levels of resilience allows us to prioritize those who need the most support when we account for student Quit Points. We can use the most resilient student as a model for the rest of the class, and plan early interventions, often through building optimism or task value, for those who are more likely to give up. Applying a personalized approach to students and the variables that positively impact their Quit Points allows educators to increase the amount of learning that takes place.

SHORT-TERM OBSTACLES

When we look at the bottom of the equation, we are looking at the types of barriers our students face that make them more likely to quit. As we've seen, short-term obstacles can begin both inside or outside the classroom. These include daily nutrition, sleep deprivation, drug use, peer drama, poor teacher relationships, and low self-esteem. It is important to recognize that these issues alone will not necessarily result in quitting but can make Quit Points more likely. To overcome these challenges, students need to provide more effort than they would otherwise show, to achieve a similar result as if there was no obstacle. Imagine a student with poor nutrition who has a stomachache from eating candy for breakfast. If the student wants to be engaged in class, it will take more energy to do the assignments while dealing with the discomfort than it would if the student was feeling well. These types of obstacles will increase the chance of students reaching a Quit Point, because it is one more hurdle to overcome.

The first three short-term obstacles (daily nutrition, sleep deprivation, and drug use) pertain to the most basic human needs found in Abraham Maslow's hierarchy. According to Maslow's research, higher levels of learning can't occur until they fulfill those physiological and safety needs. If students are hungry, tired, or under the influence of drugs (either prescription or illegal), they will have a tough time engaging in learning because they lack fulfillment of their basic needs. These obstacles indicate that something is missing that is necessary for students to be safe and healthy. Education will be, at best, a secondary priority in this situation. Until they can provide for their basic needs, these students are at increased risk of quitting.

The next three obstacles (peer drama, poor teacher relationships, and low self-esteem) relate to the mid-level needs of belonging and esteem found in Maslow's hierarchy. If a student has a conflict with a peer or teacher, that conflict can disrupt a sense of belonging and be enough to cause the student to quit. Likewise, a student who has a negative self-image is more likely to give up than a student who is confident. Students may not feel they belong in a class with peers who they perceive as "smarter." We see evidence of this type of behavior in a student "saving face" by explaining poor academic performance through "I didn't even try" rather than risking looking foolish by trying and failing.

Attempting interventions for short-term obstacles can also increase the chance of quitting if the student believes that the teacher doesn't understand that the student's stressor is related to basic psychological needs. Teachers often make the mistake of assuming individuals are misbehaving when they are more concerned with meeting their needs. Distraction, procrastination, and avoidance are easy to see, but the cause for these behaviors isn't as apparent. Applying equal treatment to a student feeling a lack of safety and one who is misbehaving can make it seem like the teacher isn't interested in either student's well-being. This approach may cause severe strain on any relationship between the teacher and student, and significantly increase the likelihood of quitting.

An example of this difference is in the use of phones during class. If students are just playing on their phones or looking at social media, they will recognize a reprimand for what it is and redirect, putting their phones away and focusing on class. But if students are receiving updates about a family situation, a difficult message from a boyfriend or girlfriend, or a friend in need of support, then a teacher who treats them as if they're misbehaving will receive a more hostile reaction. We may wish our students could handle these obstacles in a more "mature" or "adult" manner, but that is not always possible. Many students lack the skill to compartmentalize or communicate their challenges more appropriately at their age or development levels.

Sometimes acknowledging students' needs when dealing with short-term obstacles is enough to make them feel supported and understood. They may re-engage in academic work if they see that the classroom is a safe environment that values their needs. Consider the example of the student on the phone. Is it better for the student to put the phone away and make a procedural display of working while Effort Rationing? Or is it better for the student to answer a few texts from Mom before re-engaging in academic work? Some students will be more receptive to the second option, knowing they addressed a short-term need and can now focus.

Other times, students' short-term obstacles will push them too close to their Quit Points for them to be able to learn that day. Educators sometimes need to accept the reality that a short-term obstacle will impact a day's worth of learning. In that case, our goal is to start fresh the next day. As in the example above, trying to force a student through a short-term obstacle can inadvertently create a new motivation to quit. While no teacher likes losing opportunities for learning, a teacher willing to lose the battle for the day to win the war for a student's long-term learning can make an immense impact on the student.

LONG-TERM OBSTACLES

Long-term obstacles are often rooted in students' innermost circle of family and friends, or in their self-identity. Personal goals not aligned with class, unstable home life, alcohol and drug abuse, negative self-perception, antisocial or amotivated peer group, and poor attendance are examples of long-term obstacles. These factors also limit the amount of energy students can give to learning. A student with poor attendance is going to feel burdened with the pressure to catch up. But the only way the student can do that is by putting forth more effort than the rest of the group, which is already on pace. Students who are unwilling or unable to provide this extra effort will quit instead of exerting the significant effort needed to catch up.

Long-term obstacles present persistent and often severe challenges to a student's attempts at success in the classroom, but this does not necessarily result in more frequent and entrenched quitting. Sometimes students' coping mechanisms mask the impact of their problems on their academic engagement. Avoidance and withdrawal in the classroom could draw attention to problems about which they don't want teachers and peers to know. For example, a parent's drug abuse may be an obstacle students don't want to disclose to anyone except their closest friends. In this situation, they will devote significant energy to Effort Rationing because that form of quitting draws less attention to more significant problems they might try to hide.

Other students may withdraw to such a degree that classroom interventions are insufficient to prevent quitting. In these situations, students reach their Quit Points before even setting foot in the classroom. Some students suffer from chronic malnourishment and go to school primarily for the opportunity to eat breakfast and lunch. They devote so much energy to patiently waiting for food that they don't have much left for learning. They dedicate their focus exclusively

> **Distinguishing between short-term and long-term obstacles can help a teacher determine the next course of action.**

to providing for their basic needs, so the thought of academic engagement is enough to create a Quit Point. Situations such as these require building-wide support from counselors, social workers, or other community programs before students are ready to focus on academics instead of survival.

Long-term obstacles, if not successfully addressed, will lead to low academic achievement and frequent disciplinary problems. The pervasive and persistent nature of these obstacles makes suspensions, expulsions, and dropping out inevitable outcomes for students struggling with these problems. Those who experience peer conflict or low task optimism for the day are only likely to quit or Effort Ration for a short period, but those with long-term obstacles are more likely to disengage completely. Until they know they have met their basic physiological and safety needs, they may prefer the stress of failure to the pressure of trying to achieve. This situation occurs because they don't have the foundation they need to seek higher needs such as learning. Identifying the obstacles that lead to this level of quitting is the only way we can hope to support any level of consistent academic engagement.

Distinguishing between short-term and long-term obstacles can help a teacher determine the next course of action. A student under the influence of drugs or alcohol does not require the same intervention as a student who has a drug or alcohol abuse problem. One who has conflicts with peers or significant others is not necessarily the same as another who is involved in abusive relationships. A teacher can potentially manage short-term obstacles to prevent a student from reaching a Quit Point, but the pervasive and persistent nature of long-term obstacles makes it difficult for a teacher to intervene without additional support. We differentiate between these types of barriers to better understand whether there are sufficient resources in the classroom to address the situations. Any interventions designed for this group of students must go beyond what works for the broad middle of the bell curve and go the "extra mile" to impact the most severe and persistent quitting.

TEACHER TAKEAWAY

The goal of organizing the variables that influence effort and Quit Points is to provide tools and a vocabulary, so educators can address the root of quitting, rather than struggling through the symptoms that plague classrooms daily. We can positively influence a student's effort once we use the lens of quitting. This approach helps us to better understand what causes students to give up. The Quit Point equation serves as a daily reminder to treat the patient rather than the symptom.

We are in the unique business of working with children and young adults who are individuals, first and foremost. We cannot cure the problems of education by treating all students as if they suffer from the same challenges and opportunities. When educators acknowledge the realities facing students and build that into a personalized learning experience that accounts for Quit Point, we can begin to positively impact the catalysts of student optimism, task value, and resilience, while developing strategies to mitigate the negative impact of short- and long-term obstacles.

Optimism	
Limited	❑ Students do not believe they can be successful academically ❑ Students' expectations of success are based on fantasy ideals ❑ Students are only optimistic when receiving direct support
Progressing	❑ Students believe they can be successful on daily assignments ❑ Students' expectations of success are based on pragmatic goals ❑ Students are optimistic working independently
Advanced	❑ Students are highly confident in their ability to perform on major projects and tests ❑ Students' expectations of success are based on pragmatic and personal goals ❑ Students are optimistic about their ability to teach and support others

Figure 2.3: Optimism Rubric

Task Value	
Limited	❑ Students do not understand the purpose for engaging in learning activities ❑ Students' peers and family do not prioritize learning
Progressing	❑ Students understand learning is important but do not understand how daily assignments support learning ❑ Students' peers and family value academic achievement only when it relates to self-identity and extrinsic goals
Advanced	❑ Students regularly connect the value of assignments to their learning opportunities and participate regularly ❑ Students' peers and family value lifelong learning and seek out opportunities for new experiences

Figure 2.4: Task Value Rubric

Resilience	
Limited	❏ Students rarely try once they have encountered an obstacle ❏ Students respond negatively to change ❏ Students tackle obstacles individually
Progressing	❏ Students require support to continue to try after they have encountered an obstacle ❏ Students respond well to minor changes ❏ Students tackle obstacles with the assistance of close friends and teachers
Advanced	❏ Students can increase their effort on their own after encountering an obstacle ❏ Students show a willingness to adapt to change ❏ Students build new relationships in order to help overcome obstacles

Figure 2.5: Resilience Rubric

Student Obstacles	
Limited	❏ Students' stressors are based on physiological needs (nutrition, sleep, health, etc.) ❏ Students have consistent relationship problems (family, peer, teacher, etc.) that distract from their learning ❏ Students rarely have support and safety outside the classroom
Progressing	❏ Students rarely encounter stressors based on physiological needs (nutrition, sleep, health, etc.) ❏ Students rarely have relationship problems (family, peer, teacher, etc.) that distract from their learning ❏ Students' families help support stability and safety outside the classroom
Advanced	❏ Students have a support network that provides assistance to their primary caregivers in order to meet their physiological needs (nutrition, sleep, health, etc.) ❏ Students have socioemotional support to help maintain healthy relationships (family, peers, teacher, etc.) ❏ Students' family and community help support stability and safety outside the classroom

Figure 2.6: Student Obstacles Rubric

CHAPTER 3

ESTABLISHING A QUIT POINT MINDSET

Develop a mindset that limits quitting by emphasizing practice, growth, collaboration, and student ownership

"They can't pay me less than I can work."
—BULGARIAN ADAGE ATTRIBUTED TO THE
SHOPI PEOPLE OF THE BALKANS

LL PARENTS ARE familiar with the unpredictable and irrational behavior of children. Parents have come to expect that their children will refuse to eat when hungry, refuse to sleep when tired, and throw a tantrum at a moment's notice. And our youngest children aren't the only ones who exhibit this type of behavior. Teenagers are as challenging as toddlers for many parents. They might ask to go shopping, then demand that their parents stay 10 feet away the entire time, or complain that their mom never listens even though they refuse to speak to her for extended periods. This disconnect can cause frustration for all parties involved. After a while, expecting the unexpected becomes a natural part of being a parent.

Kids can be as irrational and unpredictable in school as they are at home. They might take notes during the period and then throw them away as they leave the room, or attempt to "punish" a teacher by not turning in assignments. While parents learn to deal with the unpredictable nature of their children, teachers often believe they can control these irrational behaviors by applying adult rationality. They think learning is a simple matter of going to school and following directions. The assumption is that if the instructions students receive are perfect, then their responses will be positive and predictable. This plan, however, most often results in disappointment. Just like with parenting, the logical classroom decisions teachers make don't guarantee predictable student reactions. Unless teachers keep this at the forefront of their minds, they will inadvertently supply opportunities for students to reach their Quit Points.

Some of the most exciting lessons teachers plan are projects that connect to student interests. From the teacher's point of view, it is rational to assume that tapping into students' love for music, movies, or video games will result in a great deal of student engagement. But the focus on positive potential outcomes often leads to disappointment and frustration when some students inevitably Effort Ration or completely blow off what could be a fun way to learn. The teacher becomes discouraged in much the same way a parent does after planning a family outing that results in screaming children and a disgruntled spouse. The best of intentions were met with irrational behavior from the kids, leading to discouraged adults. This result does not mean that well-planned activities don't work. It merely shows that proper planning alone does not make things fun or eliminate Quit Points.

We once saw a history project that used music to tap into student interests and spark engagement. The activity was well-prepared and had clear expectations aligned with rubrics for assessment. Students had to research and analyze lyrics related to history, then share their learning with the rest of the class. The expectations called for students to "be creative" when presenting their work. The options available included writing original music, creating a music video, or sharing a playlist. The teacher expected students to respond with engagement and enthusiasm.

Unfortunately, they were caught off guard when some students, including some who loved to talk about music, chose the irrational behavior of not even trying that part of the project. As we described in Chapter 2, many variables influence a student's Quit Point. Maybe students in the example gave up because they lost optimism when they had to perform in front of peers. Other students might have reached their Quit Point because they didn't attach any task value to the creative work. Short-term obstacles like a lack of sleep may have led to some individuals falling behind on the first day of the assignment, and then quitting because they didn't think they could catch up. Any of these factors might have prevented a student from getting to do the fun part of the project.

A rational teacher's perspective might have assumed that all these situations had simple resolutions. However, no amount of adult reasoning can prevent some students from letting emotional gut reactions lead to quitting. Planning excellent lessons and learning "funtivities" is just one part of the preparation needed to engage students.

There comes a moment when parents need to learn that they can't just follow the directions in a best-selling parenting book and be ready for every unique challenge that comes with raising a child. Only experience can teach one how to understand whether a baby is crying because she is hungry, gassy, or tired. Teachers also need to learn that their lesson plans might make sense on paper—but might not translate to student learning. They need to be as accepting and understanding of the irrationality of students as any parent, particularly when that behavior leads to quitting.

When we truly began to understand Quit Point, we developed a whole new mindset about learning in the classroom. We re-examined the perceived "keys to teaching," and started thinking about the process of learning in a whole new way.

Instead of discussing the directions we gave for assignments, we started talking about practice. The vocabulary we used to communicate achievement shifted from talking about points to talking about growth. Finally, we devoted more energy to making sure that we provided opportunities for student-led learning and collaboration. We knew these ideas were supposed to be best practices, based on the teacher training we received, but they had never quite worked. Quit Point provided the missing puzzle piece and made everything fit together.

This new mindset was the key to looking beyond what had worked in the past and facilitating learning in a new way, even when students were unpredictable or had quit. More learning occurs outside of the recommended guidelines than many teachers like to admit, such as by students who don't take notes, slack off on homework, don't study, aren't tidy and organized, and are distracted by cell phones during class. Teachers usually treat these examples like zeroes in the grade book. The assumption is that the students didn't learn anything because they didn't follow directions and complete assignments. But these teachers are prioritizing the wrong information—and failing to recognize examples of authentic learning. Looking at what happens *after* the Quit Point does not provide useful data, because the students have stopped trying to show what they know. Learning could have occurred before quitting, though, and if the student is Effort Rationing, the learning may look different than expected. For example, the "slackers" not taking notes may have paid enough attention to be able to answer spontaneous questions from the teacher, even if they aren't following the instructions the teacher has in mind.

Most teachers design lessons based on what worked in previous years, or from positive memories from when they were students. This strategy creates a problem because teachers who can only see learning that looks like they expect it to are more likely to miss learning that occurs when a student is independent or working in a "gray area" like in the examples listed above. Using the Quit Point as a guideline for shifting our mindset allowed us to see more of the learning that occurred in ways we didn't predict and changed our focus from what worked in the past to what worked for our students.

PRACTICE MAKES BETTER (NOT PERFECT)

The stereotypical image of teaching is that of an adult standing at a board telling children how to do things. This might be the steps to a math problem or daily assignment, or it could be an explanation of how to understand new content. Students then strive to follow the directions laid out by the teacher, and show their learning. But this stereotype doesn't necessarily hold true in most classrooms anymore. Education has become more collaborative, and teachers don't

> If students are practicing in class and have not yet reached a Quit Point, then they are learning. This learning won't always be a model example of mastery. It can be sloppy and incomplete, just like the notes played by a novice pianist, but it is still valuable.

always lead the class from a podium or chalkboard in the front of the room. However, one thing that hasn't changed is the culture of correction that dominates education—and how this can lead directly to students reaching their Quit Points.

Catching and correcting mistakes is an endless job for teachers. They may need to repeat directions multiple times for students who miss a step or are confused by procedures. They also scrutinize answers to questions, and correct mistakes. They post missing assignments in the classroom so students can make up work. After a while, teachers become so accustomed to catching errors that they can anticipate the mistakes students will make—and try to correct them before they happen. This situation is especially prevalent in math classes. Teachers often include mistakes students need to avoid as part of their explanation on how to solve problems. From the perspective of most educators, this culture of correction is a vital part of the learning process. But looking at how our students learn outside of school shows us that this might not be the best way.

Imagine if a child's piano teacher stopped the student every time he or she made a mistake. A wrong note, an error in hand positioning, or a shift in tempo would cause the prospective piano player to stop for correction. Even young Beethoven would have struggled to overcome the urge to quit, if he'd been subjected to this type of teaching. Constant interruptions and criticism do not build confidence! And scenarios from the world of sports are similar. Hitting a baseball is extremely difficult. World-class baseball players often swing and miss, and the best players in the world are only successful a third of the time. At first, kids are taught to hit baseballs off a tee, to make things easier, and they still may need multiple attempts to make reliable contact. Coaches don't come out onto the field, whether in T-ball or the major leagues, and correct players after every missed swing. If they did, games would take so long that players would no doubt quit at a higher rate, and many parents would give up watching before their children even had a chance to learn.

In each case, the important thing for the novice musician or athlete is that they keep practicing. Sometimes that practice must be focused and deliberate to teach precise skills. At other times, merely carrying on and maintaining effort, no matter how awkward things are, is enough. We need to apply this lesson more often in the classroom, with a mindset that emphasizes practice first and perfection second. If students are practicing in class and have not yet reached a Quit Point, then they are learning. This learning won't always be a model example of mastery. It can be sloppy and incomplete, just like the notes played by a novice pianist, but it is still valuable. Only after a student can demonstrate consistent practice in the classroom will coaching and correction lead to meaningful results.

In fact, research has shown that students of any craft need 10,000 hours of practice to perfect it. No one should expect them to be perfect the first—or second or third—time through. Instead, teachers must expect students to spend those first attempts learning through trial and error and allow the learning to happen.

What we can do is encourage deliberate practice rather than expecting immediate perfection. In doing so, we avoid the overly high expectation—and the criticism that comes with it—that leads students to grow frustrated and reach their Quit Points. Students who show consistent effort toward practice, even if it is "sloppy" or in need of correction, can be nudged into a brief period of more focused and precise effort. Even those who lack the skill or stamina to maintain deliberate practice for longer than a few minutes can show significant achievement just by focusing their effort for short bursts each day.

Small doses of productive work can add up to real gains in learning. Students who struggle with vocabulary, for instance, are more likely to Effort Ration and skip over words they don't know, rather than trying to learn new words each time they read. Demanding sustained precision in reading, and correcting every mistake, will surpass the energy they have for the task—and lead to a Quit Point. Instead of expecting perfection, a teacher should focus on brief periods and precise practice on skills the student is lacking. The teacher could ask a child to look up a word or two in a particularly relevant passage. This request creates a small yet attainable goal for even a low-optimism reader. This shift in mindset can take a task that might have led to quitting (learning new words) and turn it into a small victory of engagement and effort for that student.

Our focus on short periods of increased effort is a sharp contrast to the traditional measure of practice: time. Teachers tell students to study for X hours or work "bell to bell" because that is how most define practice. The problem is that emphasizing the time spent, instead of the moments of precision learning, encourages students to count the seconds and try to look busy, rather than focusing on learning. It inadvertently teaches students that Effort Rationing is enough to demonstrate engagement. If they look like they're following directions for the set amount of time, the teacher will assume they are focused on learning. This example is why some students complete their assignments early, but then wait to turn them in until the end of the period. Their goal is to meet a time requirement instead of showing more precision.

This new mindset allowed us to treat our students in a different way—and our students learned that they could fulfill our expectations with short periods of increased precision in their learning. Students began asking for feedback and coaching. Many students started demonstrating these short bursts daily. The temporary increase in effort took their focus away from filling or counting time and replaced those potential Quit Points with periods of increased effort.

Our mindset on practice mirrors the culture of major companies in Silicon Valley, such as Google. They are less concerned with employees working 9–5 than they are with encouraging bursts of creativity and effort. They are famous for providing ping-pong tables, nap pods, and unlimited snacks for their workers. In Google's case, the flexible atmosphere is deliberate, and aims to promote creativity, teamwork, and mental stamina. Teachers can benefit from structuring their classroom environments in a manner that does the same, facilitating work habits that contribute to student success. And students will focus on learning rather than avoiding mistakes, or just looking busy. Stressing a learning process that embraces a culture of practice, even if that practice includes mistakes, is likely to decrease students quitting.

Emphasizing practice as our daily expectation also allows

us to make individual goals for each student. Students begin by practicing independently, and their performance provides information about where they can gain the most impact from an increase in effort. Coaching facilitates short bursts of increased precision by delivering such feedback as, "Can you provide an example?" or "Can you work on capitalizing the words at the start of a sentence?" or "How does this compare to what we learned yesterday?" Rather than reviewing work for completion or to correct mistakes, we shifted to a process that addressed the Quit Point in each student. And that encouraged consistent growth and achievement for all students.

The result of adopting a culture that stresses practice is that the end goal is learning, not perfection. Emphasizing that practice is about getting better, and deliberate effort is part of elite performances, helps students understand that effort is the critical variable to their success. This culture limits the pressure on students and allows teachers to devote their energy to preventing quitting in the classroom. The result is more meaningful learning for students.

GROWTH MINDSET

Another way to shift your mindset to take Quit Point into account is to focus on something called growth mindset. We did this by taking a lesson from the research of Dr. Carol Dweck. Dweck's research juxtaposes two standard mindsets toward learning: growth mindset and fixed mindset. Individuals with a fixed mindset approach learning in absolute terms. From their perspective, answers are right or wrong, people are smart or stupid, and some people can accomplish certain tasks while others cannot. A fixed mindset reduces education to artificial markers such as grades or test scores and ignores the process that goes into any new learning. A growth mindset, on the other hand, emphasizes the effort and support needed to achieve goals and improve. This mindset results in prioritizing the process instead of the outcome.

Communicating through a fixed mindset emphasizes the option to quit because the mindset describes learning outcomes in absolute terms. "Do this or you'll fail." "I need you to put down your phone and take notes." "If you give it a chance, maybe you'll like math." These types of statements inadvertently permit

> Instead of looking at their daily tasks as work to complete and turn in, we started emphasizing feedback. Students needed to show their progress to either the teacher or a classmate, then act on immediate feedback to meet expectations.

quitting for students who lack motivation for learning. They can quit and fail, ignore the lesson and stay on their phones, or accept failure and ignore math. The options are very black and white, and right there—making it simple for the students to choose the one that is easiest for them.

By the time students reach high school, too many have learned more about quitting than about learning. From their perspective, movie day means you can give up if you're quiet, word find day means you can stop working as long as you copy off your friend, group work means you can disengage if your partner is smart or hardworking, and fun project means you can procrastinate until right before the work is due—as long as you find a way to meet the stated goal. Emphasizing fixed goals often encourages students to take shortcuts so they can quit faster and more often. They are learning to milk the system, rather than learn from it. We discovered that fixed mindsets were common in the students who most frequently quit.

Our first significant attempt at making a positive impact on quitting was to change the climate and expectations in the classroom. Our goal was to take the focus away from activities where students were already using Effort Rationing, or even quitting. Changing our expectations from absolute markers, such as "Finish your work," to growth-based norms like "Try to improve this section and check back in," shifted the focus and culture of the classroom. The average student realized it was easier to meet these new expectations than it was to find a new way to quit. For example, instead of looking at their daily tasks as work to complete and turn in, we started emphasizing feedback. Students needed to show their progress to either the teacher or a classmate, then act on immediate feedback to meet expectations.

The effect of this change was quick and powerful. Students who had previously tried to run out the clock with Effort Rationing and turn in partially completed assignments stopped telling us that they'd finished their work and started asking us what they needed to do to *improve* their work. Daily revisions became the norm instead of daily Effort Rationing.

Dweck's work shows that cognitive ability is not fixed, or solely a byproduct of intelligence or IQ. Students reach their potential through the effort they give to grow beyond their original ability. When we asked students to focus their energy and demonstrate more deliberate practice, what we meant was that they need to show growth. This expectation might mean showing a greater depth of knowledge than their initial effort, or simply clarifying their learning more explicitly. We personalized growth targets to each student so that everyone, regardless of skill level, could reach his or her full potential.

Depending on your own experience in the classroom, you've probably had students with seemingly high potential who simply did not put forth the effort needed to maximize their achievement. As they progress through their years of schooling, they eventually fall behind their peers because regular Effort Rationing has led to deficiencies over time. They grow accustomed to having higher levels of achievement than most of their peers, even though they don't always demonstrate higher levels of effort. The fixed target of "good grades" becomes their Quit Point, because they achieve this target even though they regularly quit. Meanwhile, students who routinely show high levels of effort and a mindset of learning and growth can begin to outperform their more gifted peers because their consistent growth bridges the initial gap between their relative abilities.

When teachers continually talk about points and grades, it reinforces a fixed mindset in which students know precisely when it is OK to quit. "You need to pass this class" implies that they can stop working once they earn a passing grade. "This is worth five points" insinuates only a small penalty for giving up. Instead, we emphasize the process of learning, with a focus on deliberate practice and bursts of increased effort, to eliminate achievement as an excuse for quitting. Changing our achievement expectation to reflect personal growth rather than absolute markers has helped students better understand our mindset regarding learning.

Redefining success through the lens of a growth mindset can also positively impact students' optimism. Traditional measures of success, like good grades, delay any satisfaction students might gain from their work for months at a time. All the points they earn are placeholders for that final score at the end of the grading period. It is no surprise that when students perceive school in this way, they become concerned about improving their grade only at the end of the grading period. In contrast, effort and engagement can be immediately rewarded with praise and recognition. As a teacher, what provides a greater sense of achievement and optimism: a performance evaluation at the end of the school year, or consistent peer feedback that recognizes your effort working with students? Most individuals, including children, respond better when they receive instant feedback and acknowledgment of a job well done. These rewards are especially meaningful when we prioritize them over points.

Reinforcing achievement and learning daily, instead of on a grade card, allows every day to become a chance to focus on the positive and build optimism. As discussed in Chapter 2, a lack of confidence makes it more likely that students will quit. But in a culture of growth, failure is never absolute—because students can make mistakes and still demonstrate improvement. This approach teaches them that errors are a small part of the learning process ... and increases their confidence. The traditional mindset values fixed achievement, which allows lost points, missing work, or student behaviors to drag down our students and limit their optimism. Many young students who struggle to regulate their actions are "graded" on a daily color chart. While the intent of the teacher seems rational, a student who earns a "yellow day" may lose sight of any growth made during the school day because of the fixed nature of the chart. In cases such as these, bad days or bad grades become the focus for a student and detract from real learning opportunities.

When we filtered our assignments through our new Quit Point mindset, we began to question our old habits. Did a student need to correctly answer 30 math problems if they'd coasted through the first 15? How many questions would we require a student to answer correctly to be sure they'd learned? Were we assigning work because we knew it had educational value ... or because we needed to count points to assign a grade? In the past, we assumed that everything we assigned was about the learning. As it turned out, much of it was about making our grade book look good.

What it looked like was busywork. Extra questions that gave us round point totals. Meaning many questions were unnec- essary—but got us to the point total we needed for assigning grades. Once we started addressing Quit Point, we realized that each of those filler questions increased the chance of students quitting. They did not see the point of maintaining the effort needed to complete an assignment when it looked like busywork.

We were unintentionally lowering the task value for our students by building assignments that looked the way we thought they should look, instead of building assignments that focused on actual learning.

These little pieces of busywork weren't doing anything to benefit our students' learning. They were there to make sure the scores added up correctly in our grade book. Once we realized that, we decided to stop worrying about points, and changed our assignments to emphasize growth instead. Questions didn't need numbers, because we didn't need to calculate percentages of correct responses. We increased the complexity of questions as the assignment progressed, to make sure that each assignment was about growth rather than points. This strategy meant we needed more open-ended questions instead of ones that Siri or Alexa could answer. As a result, students began to give more comprehensive responses—and we discovered that students were less likely to quit on open-ended questions than they were on questions with only one right answer.

As the frequency of quitting decreased, we realized we could improve our approach even further. We were still holding on to our old mindset about what it meant for students to be "done." Did they need to do an entire assignment to learn? If a student was engaged and showing growth, why did it matter if the student missed a question or two? Would it be better for a student to demonstrate a more extended burst of deliberate practice and leave a portion of the assignment incomplete? We realized that it didn't matter if all students attempted the same number of questions, because they didn't need to earn a point total comparable to their peers. This realization was critical to delaying Quit Points from students who became frustrated when they ran out of time. Instead of telling them they needed to finish, we could focus on the questions that would most benefit each student. We were shifting the usually fixed notion of time to one that flexibly accommodated the needs of each learner.

Now that we were no longer tied to the idea of entering 30 grades all at once, we were able to unlock the power in the word "yet," as outlined by Dweck. The flexibility of time is important within the growth mindset because people learn at different rates. If your goal as a teacher is for students to learn according to your timeline, you inadvertently strip them of their control over the situation. Are students likely to give their full effort if they believe they're going to fail at completing the task within the given time frame? Or are they more likely to give up and accept the inevitable grade that goes along with quitting? We learned to avoid these challenges by shifting our focus to growth and deliberate practice, rather than fixed timelines.

The flexibility of time became another tool we used to avoid Quit Points. We didn't need all the students to maintain the same pace and be on the same assignment—just to keep our grade book organized. This system meant that students didn't have to rush ahead to the next task to avoid falling behind. Even quitting became less of an obstacle. As much as we try to limit Quit Points, we know there are times when irrational or unpredictable behaviors will prevent learning. Our flexibility helped us make sure students could show achievement no matter the obstacle. The student hasn't failed to learn a subject; the student just hasn't mastered it yet. Struggling through learning is OK because the student has not reached the learning target yet. Reinforcing this concept instills a growth mindset that reduces the likelihood of quitting.

ASSESSMENT MINDSET

Rethinking how grades and points impacted daily assignments caused us to reconsider our mindset about assessment, as well. We knew that if classwork was accidentally leading to quitting, then testing could, too. Students have prejudices based on their experiences with quizzes, tests, projects, pre-tests, post-tests, and the wide variety of ways teachers attempt to measure learning. These prejudices can lead students to reach a Quit Point just because they know a test is coming. Anxiety and low optimism of achievement can become a part of a student's identity as a "bad test taker." Clarifying what we mean by assessment can help avoid this potential confusion and stress.

Right about the time we were beginning our study of Quit Point, our school district started to emphasize data-driven education. We met regularly with colleagues to track and discuss the results of pre-tests and post-tests, to improve instruction. This strategy was supposed to help us improve our teaching, but the Quit Points we observed suggested otherwise. Pre-tests were supposed to assess content knowledge when we were starting a new unit, so we could ensure appropriate learning targets for all students. However, it was impossible to use the data because so many students reached a Quit Point *during* pre-testing.

We were, at that time, using multiple-choice on those pre-tests, but we realized that the format made it too easy for students to quit. All they had to do was guess on every question and get to the end as quickly as possible. Most students didn't expect to be able to answer questions about unfamiliar content, and guessing became the default action on those pre-tests. It therefore became impossible to determine what students were learning, because there was no pattern to the questions that they answered correctly. Some students answered two questions correctly on the pre-test, and incorrectly on the post-test. Did those students unlearn what they knew? Did they suffer from some illness that affected their memory? Or did they just guess?

As described in Chapter 2, this was partly a problem of task value. Students couldn't see the value in tests they were supposed to score poorly on. It was also a problem with traditional assessment. Teachers assume tests show what students know. This approach makes sense when students try to do their best to score well on the test. But it's also the kind of "rational" thinking that doesn't always apply to kids. We needed a new mindset about assessment to resolve these issues.

Assessment has two primary purposes:

- Providing information (formative assessment)

- Evaluating learning (summative assessment)

But what happens when that assessment breaks down entirely—and leads kids to their Quit Point? We addressed this by establishing a new assessment mindset founded on our culture of daily practice. We didn't need a new strategy, because the practice work already provided all the data we needed. We simply shifted to open-ended questions, used students' initial levels of understanding as a baseline, and expected to see improvement as they had more opportunities to learn. The best part of this approach was that students didn't increase their chances of quitting, as they did on the pre-tests. From their perspective, they were working on typical classroom assignments and focused on growth as usual.

Anything can be a formative assessment if it provides information about students' progress toward their goals. At the end of every day, we would meet to give each other a thumbs-up or thumbs-down based on how well the co-planned lesson went. Our criteria was based on whether we felt the students showed sufficient learning to move on to the next goal ... or whether we had to continue with our original plan. Note that there was no need to mention grades or achievement. Assessment is not a section of a lesson plan, or a way to determine points in a grade book. While other teachers discussed whether their students were "doing work" or "trying hard enough," our formative assessment discussions centered around what students understood and where they needed more support. This information helped us plan lessons that provided all the necessary opportunities for students to succeed.

As our understanding of student learning changed via our focus on formative assessment, our views also shifted on summative assessment. To follow our emphasis on practice, we began to think of this type of testing as performance. Musicians and athletes practice so they can perform at their best when it matters most, and students' practice should connect to a performance, too. It was important to make sure students could authentically communicate their learning in their own words. We already had a good grasp of our students' learning from the daily formative assessment, so we focused on how well they could connect their knowledge to something else, rather than testing what they already knew.

We honed in on a greater depth of knowledge and higher-level thinking. We expected students to make comparisons, organize their learning, and relate their knowledge to personal experiences. We were initially worried that this might introduce more pressure and lead to more quitting, but we found the students to be more optimistic in this model than they were about traditional tests. We, in turn, were able to communicate more easily, which led to students having a greater awareness of their learning. We replaced assessment scores with feedback, such as "Provide comparisons to show greater depth of learning." Because we didn't give low scores, students were more confident, and no longer gave up from the frustration of poor achievement.

Students who had once guessed through multiple-choice tests or randomly filled-in answers to finish faster now spent more time showing their learning on open-response summative assessments. Students also stopped referring to themselves as "bad test takers" because they became more metacognitive. They asked for more time or more preparation because they recognized how to demonstrate their learning. We had already embraced flexibility regarding time, and it was easy to apply that idea to student performance. We no longer had concerns about cheating, because we had no multiple-choice or single-word responses. Each student might have a slightly different answer, which meant no one was copying anyone else. Best of all, we had the flexibility to offer more time to students who needed it.

Once we applied our new mindset about assessment, students' mindsets also changed. They became less stressed about taking tests, and more confident in their abilities to learn.

And we had a better idea of what our students knew—because they were less likely to quit on us before we found out.

STUDENT OWNERSHIP

The increased engagement and decreased quitting made us realize how important it was for students to own and drive their own education. Every unit, students would demonstrate learning above the level we had grown accustomed to. This growth made us more aware of the limitations of "sage on the stage" teaching. Recent efforts have emphasized more student-centered learning... but neglected to shift ideas regarding student motivation. Attempts to give students the lead through inquiry and student choice may work for motivated students, but do little for students who quit. When students quit, teachers traditionally fall back into a power dynamic that denies the student full ownership.

This approach is like the carrot-and-stick method of parenting. Children sometimes refuse to eat dinner, even when parents offer a choice of what to eat. Parents who try to motivate the child through incentives might provide extra video game time. Others who use more of a disciplinary approach might use a timeout to try to convince their child to eat. Either scenario can lead to a battle of wills if the child decides to engage in a power struggle instead of rationally weighing the options. In the end, the result is determined by whether or not the parents get their way. When this occurs, the parents are the ones determining the outcome—and the children never feel ownership over the situation.

Educators do much the same thing. Consider for a moment

a broken-down car is on the side of the road. To move the vehicle, a person may choose to push it or pull it. Pushing requires a great deal of strength, and once the individual stops pushing the car, the vehicle ceases to move. This approach is like the parent/child scenario that results in a power struggle. If an educator (or parent) tries to push a child, that child can choose to push back, and actively work against the attempts of the adult. Additionally, the adult's relationship with the child will deteriorate. If a teacher is using this sort of motivation, the student might stop coming to class altogether. The moment a teacher stops pushing, the student collapses and accepts defeat. The student has reached the Quit Point.

If one could pull a car by hand with a tow rope, it would also require a high level of energy and strength. Pulling students toward your way of thinking is less confrontational, but still requires a great deal of energy from the teacher. At the high school level, we see teachers pulling students toward the finish line as grades and graduation deadlines approach. One of our colleagues spent his entire lunch break, normally reserved for planning, to track down students who had refused to take their final exam. While this teacher only wanted his students to be successful, the students were not motivated to attempt the test, let alone prepare and do their best work. Despite the teacher's effort, most of the students still refused to take the exam. Even if they agreed to complete the test, the adult was doing the work while the students were just going through the motions.

This educator had positive intentions, but the fault of this approach is that the motivation disappears once the teacher stops pulling. Even the students who ended up taking the exam were never motivated to do their best. A few cooperated, hoping the teacher would stop harassing them, but did not give substantial effort. The result was low-level Effort Rationing, where the teacher put forth more effort to convince students to take the test than the students exerted to pass the exam itself.

> Teachers can be more flexible about timing and patient with students as their goals evolve. As children gain optimism and become more resistant to quitting, they will often redefine their goals. Over time, those goals become more aligned with what the adults are hoping for.

When teachers use their positions of power and authority to assert control over students, it does not necessarily change the students' motivations. This approach may move a small group of individuals toward the desired action, but does not qualify as real motivation, because any change in behavior is purely coercive. It will not result in sustained or long-term gains. The only way for students to keep moving toward their goals and make progress is for them to accept ownership over how their actions and habits equate to learning and reaching their desired outcomes.

A classroom culture that promotes student ownership of learning (or at least as much as possible) is one in which the teacher no longer must push or pull students toward goals. Teachers may instead empower students to define the purpose of their learning. Working toward a goal one sets for oneself is the opposite of pushing or pulling; it is the car propelling itself. It will eliminate the power struggle, which only creates an excuse for the student to quit. While not all students will choose to make progress toward their goals, a surprising number of rebellious students become much more willing to work on academic achievement when teachers allow them to set the parameters and goals of their learning.

Some educators may feel that students establish insufficient goals for achievement. But teachers can be more flexible about timing and patient with students as their goals evolve. As children gain optimism and become more resistant to quitting, they will often redefine their goals. Over time, those goals become more aligned with what the adults are hoping for.

Establishing appropriate goals, like the learning process itself, takes time. If we rush to the finish line, we may end up pushing or pulling a car with no student in it, or fall short from the exhaustion of propelling the vehicle on our own. Throughout a school year, and throughout a student's formal education, educators need to seize opportunities to empower students. Seek to develop a culture that strives for students owning their learning. Once they take the lead and can voice their own ambitions, students will demonstrate a higher resistance to Quit Points, because their experience will now have personal value.

LEARNING IS COLLABORATIVE

When students have ownership over their learning, they become more authentically engaged rather than going through the motions of school. In a classroom where students take notes, it is easy for them to Effort Ration and just scribble on a paper to seem engaged. The teachers are so focused on delivering the content that they can't see whether students are learning. It's something different when they're taking ownership of the process. The first observable difference in our classroom when students started taking ownership was how much louder it got. Instead of passively accepting content, they discussed and debated as they worked. These interactions extended beyond the classroom, too. We would sometimes post the lessons on our website the night before class, and our students got started right away, messaging each other through the night and before class to prepare. The most engaged students completed their classwork early ... and then tutored their friends. This level of social interaction made us realize that we needed to shift our mindset about collaboration, too.

Human beings are social creatures in most aspects of life and find success in both college and careers when they develop social skills that help them work with others to achieve goals. In K–12 schools, though, being social is considered a distraction or even a disciplinary problem. If you ask teachers about the most significant issues in their classrooms, many will bring up social distractions such as talking or texting. Meanwhile, when students of all ages describe what they like most about school, social aspects are usually high on the list. As we observed our most social students, we realized *they* were the ones checking assignments early to help their friends. The loud students weren't quitters; they were helping their friends succeed, too. Embracing a mindset that values these social interactions is an opportunity for educators to increase engagement and delay Quit Points.

Teachers learn from collaborating with peers, sharing ideas, and even venting about their concerns. If you take a good look around at the behaviors of teachers at your next staff meeting, you'll see there is just as much "distraction" and side conversation among adults as there is in a classroom. Those same behaviors would cause a teacher to redirect the class toward less-disruptive behavior, but principals rarely address these adult behaviors, fearing a negative reaction from the staff. Teachers may feel a need to share frustrations from a long day or ask colleagues how their families are doing—and if they don't have the opportunity to fulfill those social needs, they are likely to tune out rather than focus on the goals of the meeting.

Students have the same response in class when they can't fulfill their need for social interaction. But educators don't allow these natural social impulses in the classroom because it goes against the traditional norm of what school is, and people tend not to change when "that's the way we've always done it."

We can learn a lot from more communitarian societies, such as Japan and Finland, which we revere for their collaborative approaches to education. Some classrooms give groups of students a problem that they must solve collectively. In others, the teachers work together to improve lesson planning through observation and feedback. Even in the United States, there are specific models of teaching that stress collaboration, and some of the most prestigious university programs, such as Yale Business School, develop teams in which students take the same classes, and expect students to work with and learn from each other. But what about K–12? We decided to find out.

Adopting a more collaborative mindset helped us learn more about how students learn so we could provide valuable collaborative support for those at higher risk of quitting.

Keep in mind that collaboration does not mean group work. Everyone can recall a teacher assigning students to groups and giving out roles ranging from presenter to scribe. These are not fond memories, because many groups resisted collaborating as a team, and instead fulfilled separate tasks only loosely linked through a common topic. Dependable students performed the roles that required the most work, knowing they would not let the rest of the group down. Meanwhile, the structure of the group encouraged other students to Effort Ration their way through less demanding roles. For example, a timekeeper can participate with minimal learning. We sometimes hear students discuss group roles based on how easily they can Effort Ration their participation. One student who was assigned the responsibility of summarizer bragged to his friends because he "finessed the system" and "doesn't have to do anything." He was happy to take the role because he believed it would allow him to quit on most of the activity.

This method of group work is not genuinely collaborative, and just leads to individual tasks pieced together like a puzzle. The technique even earned the name "Jigsaw." This traditional method emphasizes the individualistic nature of the assignment. Teachers must facilitate an environment that encourages social learning and makes all students part of the learning process and true collaboration. Google breaks this down as a culture that gives everyone proportional responsibilities, makes sure they feel comfortable contributing, and gives everyone a chance to add value to the larger group. When collaboration is just an occasional activity, it doesn't meet these standards. Instead of working together, students will be more likely to quit and find a way to complete their collaborative expectations with minimum effort.

Genuine collaboration should be all-encompassing—and include student ownership. Instead of sitting and passively learning from the all-knowing teachers, students must be able to learn from each other, sharing their thoughts on content and developing strategies to communicate their learning. When a student does not understand the material, the default should not be to penalize them or force them to approach the teacher. Does it matter if the student learns from the teacher in a traditional manner ... or from a peer who has another way to convey the information? If the goal is learning and student growth, a healthy classroom culture should allow that learning to take place in a range of different places and ways.

Since we opened up the culture of our classrooms to reflect a collaborative climate, we have focused on student collaboration that happens organically. We stress teams rather than groups, allow them to form naturally with student input, and rely heavily on student leadership rather than teacher-driven organization. An example was a group of accelerated students who began sharing ideas for an upcoming essay through a group chat. One student brought it up hesitantly, fearing punishment for "cheating." Instead, we praised the students for owning their learning, sharing ideas that involved all the students, and creating a genuine academic discussion with the goal of improving everyone's work. The students became empowered, enjoyed tutoring peers, and reviewed things together to refine everyone's writing.

By removing the stigma on collaboration, we encouraged

high-level academic discussion and peer review. Encouraging collaboration as part of learning can empower students and result in social interactions that bridge obstacles that can lead to quitting. Working individually, these students had to face their Quit Points alone. Working together, they were able to demonstrate some of the highest levels of learning we experienced in our careers.

SOMETIMES, PUNTING IS THE BEST PLAY

Jim Tressel coached the Ohio State Buckeyes football team from 2001–2010, amassing a ridiculous win/loss record of 106–22, including three National Championship games and one National Championship victory. With a winning percentage over 80 percent in major college football, you would think he would have won over most fans. However, Tressel's style of play (known as "Tressel-ball") was slow and methodical. It relied on great defense and an offense that sometimes played cautiously to avoid losing the game. In fact, Tressel's favorite play was said to be the punt because it prevented mistakes and put his defense in a more favorable position. Many people complained that the punt was an example of quitting, and that the coach wasn't giving the players a chance to win.

But Tressel wasn't giving up or quitting on the team when he "played it safe" and punted. He was focusing the efforts of the team in a more strategic way to keep them in a position where they were always optimistic about their chances. If the players had expended too much energy on unfavorable circumstances, they would have had less ability to perform when the odds were in their favor.

We transferred this same strategic thinking about effort

to the classroom to decrease how often students had a reason to quit.

Each day presents opportunities for optimism to waver, and many of those variables are beyond our control. Think of all the situations that can occur. A driver may cut you off, the weather could be unpleasant, a traffic light can turn red and make you late, or the Wi-Fi may go out at work. Seemingly trivial events or circumstances can derail even our best efforts and become obstacles that lead to quitting. How we as teachers control our responses to these situations will help to determine how quickly students reach their Quit Points.

If teachers try to exert extra control over unpredictable occurrences and force an unrealistic result, it makes them seem unreasonable to students. To use the football analogy, trying to score on fourth down with 30 yards to go is not the easiest way for a coach to gain the confidence of the players. A mindset that sees "punting" as part of the process—instead of as quitting—understands that strategic thinking is essential to getting the best possible result. This approach allows an educator to approach each day, each class, and each lesson with the goal of identifying the best possible outcome. This way students start each day with a clean slate (or to continue the football analogy, another set of downs). Knowing that we sometimes need to cut down an assignment, modify questions, or give students a break doesn't encourage quitting. It shows that students can trust us to put each one of them in a position to be successful.

As we continue to build our classroom culture and mindset around Quit Point, our "punt day" approach has helped us maintain productive days, even when something goes wrong. Teachers quickly learn that not every day is equal in terms of student effort, focus, and production. Classroom holiday parties, for example, affect the culture of the classroom and make a climate that is better suited to excitement and optimism than assessment. Students who are excited about the fun part of the day will be more likely to quit if the teacher tries to shift their focus to something more demanding. Likewise, the day after trick-or-treating will not be as productive as a standard school day, because students are more interested in discussing their candy haul from the previous night. Almost every day offers opportunities for learning both content and skills, but teachers must expect different levels of engagement from their students and take that into account when planning lessons.

At the high school level, the same thing applies to different days throughout the school year. The entire "spirit week" leading up to homecoming will be difficult when it comes to bell-to-bell engagement. As an experienced educator, you should expect wound-up students, quite likely walking into your class with an Effort Rationing mindset. This does not imply that a teacher should give up on a day's worth of teaching and learning. On the contrary, the goal of "punting" is to limit the opportunities for students to quit. If you are fully prepared to turn expected days of reduced effort into small windows of learning, you can minimize the negative impact of students shutting down completely. This approach provides a clean slate the next day, when engagement might be better.

Teachers can also "punt" by assigning something unexpected to prevent student Quit Point. In this way, students get a chance to try an assignment outside the norm and increase their engagement. We once tried a holiday-themed writing assignment before winter break. The task was challenging because it asked the students to apply appropriate evidence in support of their claim. While we were cautious about giving an assignment that would elicit Effort Rationing, our outside-the-box expectations resulted in students showing significant effort. We were proud to see that while other classes watched movies, our students debated which person had the best thesis. The strategy focused student effort toward a productive goal, and we observed significantly less quitting than expected, based on previous experiences with days before vacation.

TEACHER TAKEAWAY

The immediate takeaway here is that learning begins with the right mindset. If that mindset focuses on grades, test scores, "right" answers, compliance, and passive learning, the result will, unfortunately, look precisely like most schools across the country. Teachers will focus on the disappointing behaviors students exhibit instead of examples of achievement. They will keep trying to make school look the way they remember, instead of adjusting to the changing needs of all students.

Educators can embrace a culture that accounts for Quit Point, consider practice to be part of the educational process, and focus on student learning and growth. This mindset is less reliant on grades and test scores and strives to make learning a collaborative process in which the students can take ownership. This mindset is the key to transforming schools to look more like what we would want for our kids. It is also the key to making teaching a job that replaces frustration with fulfillment.

Practice and Assessment Culture	
Limited	❑ Students expect to achieve learning targets immediately ❑ Students believe mistakes represent failure ❑ Students only pay attention to their grades after assessments ❑ Students are only interested in doing enough work to get a grade they desire
Progressing	❑ Students understand learning sometimes requires multiple attempts ❑ Students are not frustrated when they make minor mistakes ❑ Students solicit feedback after their assessment grades do not meet their expectations ❑ Students expect to earn good grades for completing assignments
Advanced	❑ Students dedicate consistent effort in order to refine and improve learning ❑ Students learn from mistakes in order to deepen their understanding ❑ Students concentrate on how they can improve instead of their score from assessments ❑ Students understand that achievement is based on mastery of the learning targets

Figure 3.1: Practice and Assessment Culture Rubric

Student Mindset	
Limited	❑ Students do not believe they can improve ❑ Students believe most assignments are busywork
Progressing	❑ Students believe improvement is based more on teacher effort than personal effort ❑ Students believe that assignments are important if they have a high impact on their grades
Advanced	❑ Students believe they can improve based on their effort ❑ Students don't worry about grades while working on assignments

Figure 3.2: Student Mindset Rubric

Student Ownership	
Limited	❏ Students are motivated solely through teacher intervention ❏ Students believe learning takes place solely through teacher direct instruction ❏ Students do not ask questions unless they are prompted
Progressing	❏ Students require teacher intervention before taking ownership ❏ Students recognize learning does not always require the supervision of a teacher ❏ Students ask clarification questions
Advanced	❏ Students are motivated by intrinsic goals ❏ Students create and pursue personal learning goals ❏ Students ask questions that extend their learning

Figure 3.3: Student Ownership Rubric

Collaborative Learning	
Limited	❏ Students work independently on assignments ❏ Students believe collaboration has more drawbacks than benefits
Progressing	❏ Students will collaborate with peers when prompted by teachers ❏ Students believe collaboration is beneficial as a means to making assignments easier
Advanced	❏ Students initiate collaboration with peers as a means to improving their learning ❏ Students recognize the social and academic benefits from working in a student-led group

Figure 3.4: Collaborative Learning Rubric

PART II

USING QUIT POINT STRATEGIES

CHAPTER 4

LIMITING QUIT POINTS THROUGH DIFFERENTIATION

Prevent quitting through better planning and resource design

> "*Personalization... is a chance to differentiate at a human scale, to use behavior as the most important clue about what people want and more important, what they need.*"
> —SETH GODIN

TRYING TO ACCOUNT for the individual needs of diverse learners is one of the most significant challenges for educators. Even when teachers use dynamic resources and offer active learning opportunities, some students will be bored or fall behind. We all learn differently, and our success in the classroom is dependent on how well teachers can account for these variances. Learning disabilities, physical health, and individual learning habits also impact the success of a lesson. These variables can make it seem like every student requires a distinct lesson plan or personal tutor—a level of personalization that isn't realistic in the average classroom. The result is that teachers try to incorporate strategies that can adjust for the needs of as many students as possible.

All teachers learn about differentiation and are trained to attempt it. But most find it difficult to practice on a daily basis. Instead, most classrooms use a standardized approach that aims for the middle, in hopes of reaching the largest target audience. This model, however, results in some students "slipping through the cracks." One of the best ways to address this is to differentiate between students based on individual learning styles, like providing opportunities for visual learners to learn in ways that are different from auditory learners. Other methods of differentiation sort students based on perceived skills. Many schools track students from elementary through secondary education, for that exact reason. Other schools steer students into accelerated or remedial classes based on factors such as standardized test scores. Sometimes it seems like all students need private lessons to meet their needs.

During our studies, we discovered that differentiation could be easier than most teachers assumed—and that our own differentiation model needed to change. Quit Point helped us recognize the personal nature of effort in learning, and once we realized that, we also used it to build a more personalized learning environment. Our primary strategy was to differentiate to improve student optimism, task value, and resiliency. To accomplish this, we developed a tiered model of differentiation with blueprinting to plan for individual differences and design user-friendly resources. We used our experiences with Quit Point to refine the differentiation, instead of using learning styles or skill-based divisions. We found that it helped us increase student optimism, engagement, and learning.

> A one-size-fits-all approach was the default practice in large-scale formal education. Teachers believed the system was working because most students could succeed with a standardized curriculum. But these students didn't necessarily flourish.

TIERING: ONE SIZE DOES NOT FIT ALL

What if every patient who walked into a doctor's office with a fever received the "best practice" treatment for that ailment? The doctor would give every patient a standard dose of aspirin or acetaminophen, and send the patient on his or her way. For the majority of patients, that small dose of medicine would be enough to limit the fever while their bodies fought off whatever minor illness they'd contracted. Some people would argue that helping 90-plus percent of patients was a success.

Unfortunately, this one-size-fits-all approach creates problems. The treatment only masks symptoms to make the disease more tolerable for the patient. And that can lead to more significant problems because it's neglecting the underlying illness that is causing the fever in the first place. When the treatment doesn't address the real issues, it endangers the patients with more serious diseases.

That same one-size-fits-all approach was the default practice in large-scale formal education. Teachers believed the system was working because most students could succeed with a standardized curriculum. But these students didn't necessarily flourish. Many simply tolerated the system because they saw school as a stepping stone to something important, like college or a career. And though most educators and students accepted the status quo as "good enough," some eventually started wondering why so many students were left behind.

In fact, it should come as no surprise that students dropped out and failed because the one-size approach to learning was never designed to help all students. Schools removed students from the system or quarantined them to alternative schools if they threatened the achievement of peers who were more likely to succeed. They expelled students, tracked them into remedial programs, or forbid them from attending. Then, as the culture of education evolved, people began expecting schools to provide for all students, regardless of their disabilities or disinterests. This led to programs that supported all students in their learning, including special education programs, the exploration of alternative approaches to discipline, and government funding to support struggling schools. These strategies successfully addressed more students' needs... but also exacerbated the problems of the one-size-fits-all approach. Teachers now had an even greater diversity of students, and did not have a reliable strategy for ensuring that all students would grow. Teachers had problems with student apathy.

Education had built programs for students who were falling through the cracks. And those problems weren't reaching the students the way they were supposed to.

This is why we started using our Quit Point focus and multi-tiered model. We started with the Quit Point variables of optimism and task value because we found those to be more accurate markers for individual students. And we made sure the model was flexible. We often saw students moving up a level (or two) during the year due to improved skills, work habits, and achievement goals, and made sure that this was conceivable within our model. We based our student assessments and tier assignments on a combination of student work habits, motivation, and peak ability. The system we ended up with provided an achievement, intervention, and motivation model that gave teachers a better chance to reach all students, rather than just the majority.

We do not use tiers as a ranking. Instead, we use our multi-tiered model to organize appropriate types of assignments based on the levels of learning that students demonstrate. This system allows them to feel comfortable increasing their effort and extending their learning because they focus on attainable goals regardless of their general ability. At the start of the year we assess students' skill levels and willingness to exert effort—as well as their individual Quit Points. This data tells us how much intervention each will need as we move on to new content. Once we've established each student's baseline ability and risk of quitting, we can determine which tier best suits each student's learning needs.

We use three tiers to differentiate our students. Tier 1 refers to students who are not on track to make adequate yearly progress. Tier 2 students are on track to show proficiency and advance to the next levels of education. Tier 3 students demonstrate advanced skills, comprehension, and interests in a subject area. They would benefit from learning opportunities at higher skill levels. These tiers do not refer to abilities, and students can and will change tiers throughout the year, depending on their specific needs. The tiers do, however, allow us to provide for the needs of diverse learners, and reduce quitting in our students.

IDENTIFYING STUDENT NEEDS THROUGH TIERS

Tier 1

The Tier 1 student demonstrates consistently low effort in the classroom. These students sometimes have lower abilities than their peers, due to their consistently poor engagement. Our differentiation focuses on the variables that might prevent this student from quitting, as a means for improving academic achievement and ability. A Tier 1 student generally has lower optimism than his or her peers because over time, a consistently lower effort leads to negative academic consequences. Students' failure becomes a self-fulfilling prophecy as decreasing optimism results in less productivity, less learning, and falling behind. This tier is recognizable by its low expectations for achievement, overdependence on assistance from the teacher, or cheating.

Students identified as having Tier 1 attributes usually reach their Quit Point in the early part of class. The problem can be so severe that they walk into class having already given up. Despite the "best practices" label by administrators, traditional lesson starters such as essential questions, learning targets, or class directions can accelerate these students toward their Quit Point because they feel they will fall behind. Low optimism makes it difficult for these students to process multi-step directions without assistance. Learning targets serve as a reminder that they do not feel prepared to perform as well as their peers.

Students in this group often demonstrate amotivational behaviors. When they participate in classroom activities, they rarely achieve personal goals. If they can articulate any purpose at all, it is usually an abstract concept they think the teacher wants to hear, such as "good grades" or "do my work." These students often don't even know what their goals are. Quitting might be the primary goal, because they hope it will deflect the teacher's attention enough to provide a safe withdrawal. And since they don't feel motivated to participate, even students who can achieve success will struggle to do so. The combination of consistently low productivity and amotivational behavior prevents Tier 1 students from higher achievement.

Teachers must address these students' reasons for quitting before engaged learning can occur, and teachers can make an immediate impact by ensuring that the students' initial reactions to class are less negative than they might have been. Even slight increases in optimism can impact how much the student values the learning. A quick, positive start to class might be the deciding factor in whether that student shows any effort at all throughout the lesson.

Tier 2

Tier 2 students do not have the alarmingly low effort and lack of optimism of their Tier 1 peers. Tier 2 students tend to understand how to "play school," and are therefore more likely to appear engaged and active in learning. They will continue to show progress through each school year, making them less likely to receive interventions or personalized learning opportunities. If a Tier 2 student does not exhibit concerning behaviors, the student's compliance can make it easy to Effort Ration and fly under the radar. Teachers expect to devote a great deal of time and energy to students who fall into Tier 1, but Tier 2 students also need specific strategies to prevent them from settling for regular Effort Rationing and more frequent quitting.

The behaviors of Tier 1 students often prevent teachers from recognizing that Tier 2 students are also quitting. Most Tier 1 procrastination and distraction occurs early in the lesson, requiring immediate intervention—which results in less attention paid to Tier 2 students, who tend to quit in the middle of the lesson. Their Quit Point occurs after they have engaged enough to feel confident about reaching their achievement goals. At this point, they will start performing at the bare minimum, or leaving things incomplete.

Failing to recognize this will increase the opportunities for otherwise compliant students to begin Effort Rationing. Because Tier 2 students quit differently than their peers, different interventions are needed. These students may even complete their assignments despite reaching a Quit Point, yet fail to demonstrate the skills and depth required to show growth. Teachers need to observe student work to understand when students begin their Effort Rationing, and how to motivate these students toward growth.

Tier 2 students are often externally motivated, but struggle to understand the value of any task that doesn't directly translate to points, a grade, or some other reward. Since they focus so much on how to achieve external goals, these students limit their effort to the narrow confines of what the directions expect. They are less willing to show initiative on creative assignments or provide depth in responses. When achievement and rewards stop matching the students' expectations, they will lose motivation. This problem is because of their over-reliance on external motivators. They focus more on the teachers' actions than their own when things don't go according to plan. When they quit, they will usually complain about fairness before they try to increase their effort. Improvement often comes in small increments in Tier 2, because the students need to start internalizing their goals and motivations before they can understand the importance of improved engagement.

Teachers can help those small gains turn into tremendous growth by providing appropriate feedback and support to these students. Our goal should be to reach a point where Effort Rationing becomes the exception instead of the rule.

Tier 3

The Tier 3 student is the most difficult to identify. These students usually have positive experiences in school, due to being able to achieve beyond the teacher's academic expectations.

They are not just optimistic about getting through school like their Tier 2 peers but are often confident of doing well academically because their past experiences reinforce their academic success. This expectation can lead these students to resist teacher feedback and support. They are accustomed to positive feedback, thanks to their ability to outperform their peers, and they avoid situations that can result in adverse outcomes or correction. Whereas Tier 2 students focus on directions as their guide to success, this group prefers to skip the instructions and expects to succeed based on their past achievements or superior abilities.

This independent streak can result in increased creativity, as well as increased conflict and quitting when the students fail to understand the importance of specific procedures. Since they've learned to be successful without teacher support, they may choose to give up instead of admitting they need help, or they may struggle more than their peers. Every year, we see multiple students who breezed through grades K–8, yet they reach their Quit Point the moment school gets tough. Tier 3 quitting is not as predictable as the early-lesson quitting of Tier 1, or mid-lesson quitting of Tier 2. It can manifest itself in Effort Rationing, as they attempt to demonstrate to themselves and others that they do not need to exert the same effort as their peers to complete assignments. It may also result in avoidance, where they opt to direct their energy toward other work while neglecting the task in front of them.

These students are incredibly confident about taking independent action in the classroom, and whether they reach their Quit Point or not is the critical factor in determining whether this independence leads to superior learning… or more creative quitting. For these reasons, Tier 3 students need interventions that don't restrict the freedom they expect in the classroom. Allowing for significant student autonomy encourages these students to take more ownership over their learning and avoid obstacles that lead to quitting.

Tier 3 students are intrinsically motivated, and will favor personal goals over class goals, unless the teacher makes a conscious effort to show overlaps between the two. Their strong independent streaks often require educators to provide for a great deal of freedom to avoid conflict and power struggles. These students are not necessarily high achievers and may choose to perform at a lower level if they don't see value in classroom activities. Establishing a positive relationship and learning about their individual goals are the first steps to avoiding unnecessary Quit Points for Tier 3 students. Mutual trust and understanding are needed for the teacher to feel confident about providing the autonomy these students need to feel optimistic and empowered. If conflict becomes the basis of the student and teacher relationship, quitting will occur more frequently.

> When we begin planning a unit, we consider the needs and concerns of students in all tiers so that we can provide growth opportunities and limit quitting.

Student Traits	
Tier 1	Students struggle significantly to perform at grade level, leading to low optimism. Resiliency is often low because setbacks in learning seem even larger due to deficiencies in academic progress. Effort is consistently low, resulting in low engagement and lost learning opportunities. Students in this tier typically respond poorly to types of external motivation and struggle to understand how classroom goals are personally beneficial.
Tier 2	Students demonstrate the ability to perform at grade level expectations and are on track to show proficiency in a timely manner. They are confident of earning average grades and progressing through the academic system as expected. Effort is a big indicator of determining if this student remains at a proficient level or potentially moves to higher levels of academic growth. Students are often reliant on specific instructions on how to meet these goals.
Tier 3	Students perform above proficient expectations. Their academic optimism is often higher than their peers due to reinforced high achievement. They may have resiliency at or slightly lower than their Tier 2 peers because of less school-related setbacks. Effort will usually be a key element if these students are to consistently perform above proficiency and show growth beyond standard expectations. Students in this tier are internally motivated to reach personal academic goals and engage when classroom goals align with their personal goals.

Figure 4.1: Understanding the obstacles and goals of different types of students is necessary for differentiation to be most effective.

BUILDING A TIERED CLASSROOM

Our takeaway from understanding tiers is that we need to plan our instruction in a way that builds optimism, facilitates feedback, and encourages independent exploration. Use your unit planning and lesson planning to reach these goals and adopt a more student-friendly approach to assignments. Doing so will help you delay and prevent Quit Points.

EDUCATIONAL BLUEPRINTING:
PLANNING WITH PURPOSE

Over the years, educators' priorities shifted to emphasize higher-level thinking, more in-depth knowledge, and creativity as a response to access to information through technology. Blueprinting is the strategy we use to assess learning of various depths and complexity. It also helps us to plan and organize support and interventions for students in each tier. When we begin planning a unit, we consider the needs and concerns of students in all tiers so that we can provide growth opportunities and limit quitting.

Curriculum designers McTighe and Wiggins founded blueprinting in the backward design they advocated in their book *Understanding by Design*. The concept calls on educators to plan curriculum by starting with measurable goals, which will be subject to summative assessment. Keeping the end goal in mind, teachers can work backward to determine which specific content, skills, and resources they will use in individual lessons. Shouldn't the destination be known before the journey starts? Backward planning helps teachers focus their instruction and prepare students for assessments.

We adapted this planning model and used the Quit Point needs of students in each tier. Our educational blueprinting starts with the summative assessment, much like the concept of backward design. Our goal was for students to move beyond a low-level recall of information and toward higher levels of understanding. Blueprinting gives instructors a guide for designing a curriculum that meets the instructional needs of different learners. It also helps them maximize the potential growth of each student. It expands on the backward design method by allowing more personalized instruction, using a hierarchy of foundational skills as the target for each tier's increased depth of knowledge. This strategy enables teachers and students to emphasize growth throughout the unit, as student foundational skills develop. Focusing on the needs of each tier allows teachers to plan for the moments at which students are most prone to quit.

We began to explore the possibilities of blueprinting during a routine collaboration between sessions at a professional conference. Our goal was to identify a Tier 1-level question that wasn't about specific content knowledge. We brought other teachers into the discussion, and everyone we met struggled with this task. We realized, given the unexpected difficulty we were having to identify such a question, that there was a good chance our tests were biased toward other tiers.

At that point, we started evaluating our units to see how well we differentiated the types of learning expected of our students. Unfortunately, most did not have an appropriate balance of questions for students at all levels. Some overemphasized low-level knowledge and had limited chances for independent exploration, which would increase the chances of Tier 3 students quitting. Others weighted questions toward higher-level skills, putting Tier 1 students at a disadvantage due to their lower optimism.

It was the top and the bottom groups that were most often missing growth opportunities. We were surprised by how many new questions we had to create to appropriately assess and prepare all students for growth in every unit. Despite our prior attempts to differentiate through accommodations, modifications, remedial practice, and enrichment opportunities, we found that we didn't have sufficient resources for Tier 1 and Tier 3 questions until we began blueprinting. The overemphasis of evaluating students only on specific content knowledge and the relative newness of individualized instruction naturally led teaching to focus on the middle, and we had fallen right into that trap.

It's no wonder Tier 1 students often quit at the start of class. There were days when we asked them to work on tasks that were at a level that made it impossible for them to be optimistic. They would look at their assignment and reach an immediate Quit Point, based on the difficulty of the reading or complexity of the questions. We thought these assignments would prepare them for the end-of-unit assessment. However, because the test mostly had Tier 2 and Tier 3 questions, all of our lessons were imbalanced.

Blueprinting allowed us to see that, and plan for all assessments to be at the appropriate level for all students. This approach shifted the focus of our lessons and helped eliminate multiple opportunities for quitting through a simple planning strategy.

Unit 2: Industrialization and Progressivism Blueprint Standard 10:		
The rise of corporations, heavy industry, mechanized farming and technological innovations transformed the American economy from an agrarian to an increasingly urban industrial society.		
Approaching Proficiency	**Proficient**	**Mastery**
Explain the differences between agricultural farm work and industrial factory work.	Explain how machine production improved production and created problems for industrial workers.	Evaluate how workers and entrepreneurs did not share equally from the benefits and problems that came from technology advances in manufacturing.
Skills:	**Skills:**	**Skills:**
Identify Define Give Examples	Compare Interpret Recognize cause and effect	Connect Synthesize Analyze

Figure 4.2: This sample educational blueprint ensures that we account for different student skills and abilities while addressing the learning standards of each unit. Students at various levels of proficiency are expected to demonstrate their progress on the learning standard in different ways.

We organize our blueprints according to year-long themes and skills, to build upon prior content and skills, and to overlap content standards. This helps us focus our planning process to include all the personalized needs of various learners at various skill sets. During a school year, it is easy for teachers to become distracted by the daily grind, which includes so much more than just planning. In between grading, conferences, meetings, tutoring, and other administrative expectations, teachers can ignore quality planning in favor of easier and less effective methods. Having a ready blueprint keeps us prepared and ensures that we can shift the focus of our lessons to whatever tier needs more support at that moment. For example, exploration can be the focus on days when Tier 3 students show the most quitting.

Having a blueprint ensures that our assessments are balanced—and allows us to be flexible with our lessons, depending on which students are engaged at any given time, and which are not.

LESSON PLANNING: A DAILY DOSE OF OPTIMISM

The typical lesson plan focuses on managing class time. Teachers monitor for engagement and staying on task while circulating the room. The objective is to achieve the learning targets for the day. This type of lesson looks effective to outside observers, due to the amount of activity and energy demonstrated by the hardworking teacher. Unfortunately, the better we understood Quit Point and the various needs of each tier of students, the more we discovered that standard lesson plans failed to address many key variables. We needed to build optimism, provide supports to move students out of regular Effort Rationing, and allow the space some students needed to feel empowered and independent. In the average lesson plan, teacher effort and engagement do not necessarily correlate to student effort and participation. Without attention to the variables that impact quitting, teacher effort will not be enough to result in increased student engagement.

To better prioritize the needs of our students, we began to

organize our lessons in three parts: optimism building, feed-back/growth, and independent exploration. Every day starts with a focus on optimism. We want every student to come into our room and know they will be able to succeed, regardless of any relative skill deficiencies or challenges they've faced in the past. This strategy helps Tier 1 students start class with a higher level of optimism than usual. It's easy for students to feel like they are falling behind just as class is beginning if their initial task seems complicated or confusing. To prevent these factors from leading to Quit Points, we try to make sure the first task is something every individual can complete, either independently or with peers. We designed the first part of the lesson to take five to 10 minutes at the most, so students can feel a daily boost of optimism as they transition into their primary goals.

The feedback portion is the most substantial part of the lesson. Our goal is to design learning activities that encourage growth and authentic engagement. This approach is particularly important for Tier 2 students, who have a habit of Effort Rationing because they prioritize completing

> When educators don't take the time to create visually appealing assignments and resources, students can have an adverse first reaction to their tasks. Correcting this oversight leads to one of the easiest ways to avoid Quit Points.

assignments over understanding the learning. We may ask for clarification on a written response, an incorporation of more vocabulary terms, or quotations from readings as supporting evidence. All students receive feedback that is appropriate within their tiers. This strategy can result in students showing more authentic engagement on the targeted part of the task, instead of quitting halfway through. Using direct and immediate feedback to nudge students closer to more authentic engagement leads to more substantial gains in learning over time and limits the impact of Quit Points for all students.

Independent exploration is the final part of our lesson structure. The goal is to provide time for students to take ownership of their learning, while allowing them space to connect their individual experiences to our daily goal. This strategy is particularly useful for Tier 3 students, who are intrinsically motivated. They can prioritize their interests over the topics selected by the teacher. Research, multimedia such as video and images, or presentations of learning are common goals for this part of the lesson. Exploration time not only benefits the highest achiever, but also at-risk students, who can receive additional support while their peers have the opportunity to be more independent. Trusting students to take ownership of their learning limits the chance of conflicts with high-achieving students and decreases the likelihood of quitting. These students usually value the freedom to express themselves, and struggle when they need to communicate based solely on teacher expectations. Showing a willingness to listen to their interests can be enough to limit quitting, because it proves that the teacher values their ideas.

RESOURCE DESIGN: MAKING SCHOOL "CUSTOMER FRIENDLY"

Once we've tiered our long-term planning through blue-printing and ensured that our lessons support the needs of all students, we focus on the final step of the tiering process: redesigning our resources. The key components still concentrate on building optimism, providing feedback and growth opportunities, and allowing independent exploration, but we also work to incorporate student-friendly design elements. Some may think visual appeal and presentation are trivial compared to the vital work of teaching and learning. After all, the responsibilities of assessing, grading, and facilitating educational experiences don't necessarily leave time for educators to worry about the visual presentation of every assignment and resource. However, when educators don't take the time to create visually appealing assignments and resources, students can have an adverse first reaction to their tasks. Correcting this oversight leads to one of the easiest ways to avoid Quit Points.

Engagement, motivation, and learning don't occur purely in the mind, just like our enjoyment from eating isn't something that comes solely from taste. Cooking competitions and restaurant critics judge visual appeal and presentation when evaluating the quality of a dish. They understand that we first experience food by assessing how it looks, and creative plating can add significant motivation and interest for diners. The fast-food industry emphasizes the visual appeal of their food so successfully that customers happily purchase food that bears little resemblance to what they saw in commercials. Instead of reaching a Quit Point and throwing the food away due to differences from the advertised appearance, customers are sufficiently motivated to eat and enjoy the food that they first "tasted" with their eyes.

Educators all have experience with examples of poorly designed educational resources. Elements such as low printing quality, papers crowded with a small font, or a loud thud from a thick packet hitting a desk are enough for some students to reach an immediate Quit Point. Procrastination and distraction are more likely to occur when students have a negative reaction to the appearance of an assignment. This response may be due to a drop in optimism over a task that will require more effort than the student anticipated. Many of these visual obstacles occur because the teacher prioritized their needs over those of the students. Trying to fit more text onto a page for faster, more efficient copies, or using a pre-made form designed by other teachers or textbook companies, are the types of issues that lead to this problem.

We should recognize that our students are our customers, and that we need to present the learning in a way that is favorable to them. Our students can carry over the first "taste" of engagement from a lesson, with both positive and negative outcomes. Students will struggle to focus on their learning goals if they have an unpleasant initial reaction to an assignment. Conversely, customer-friendly presentation can provide enough motivation for some students to engage in tasks that would otherwise cause stress. Solving math problems can be a daunting task and seeing a paper with only three questions instead of 30 might be the difference between a student deciding to try and a student quitting. To help create a better first impression for students, we tried to take a lesson from the things they enjoy.

Students' use of technology provides an excellent template for what kind of presentation and interface they prefer. Our design process started with incorporating visual concepts from popular phone and tablet apps, video games, and recent software. One of the first things we did was to scrap our class website in favor of a simple homepage that resembled a cell phone. The thought process was that even our toddlers navigated phones without adult help, so a similarly designed web page should be more accessible for high school students. We deleted our typical teacher website, which was full of assignments and resources, and replaced it with six icons. The result was simple, intuitive, and user-friendly. Our old site gave students an excuse to Effort Ration because they could wait 10 minutes or more before asking what they were supposed to be doing.

Our new website puts the directions in their hands. We joke with our students that there are only six icons to click, and that they can only be wrong five times, at most, before stumbling upon the assignment for the day.

| Daily Assignment | Daily Challenge | Past Assignments |

| Vocabulary | Essentials | News |

Figure 4.3: We designed our class website to prevent Quit Points by using a simple layout that is familiar to students who regularly use technology on phones and tablets.

While the class website is a starting point for all lessons, it is just a small way in which we incorporated design into our classroom model. We applied the same principles to our daily classwork. One way we shifted to a more tech-friendly presentation was to change the layout of our online assignments. Most texts are printed in a portrait layout, oriented with a shorter width and longer height to the paper. This style is what we're accustomed to with written texts, but the format does not translate as well to the technology used today. Televisions, computer screens, and smartphones are all designed in a wide-screen landscape format. We modified assignments in that format to adapt to student preferences... and noticed an immediate reduction in Quit Points. Students told us they liked not having to scroll up and down as much to view their work.

We also try to mirror the simple, clean, and high-contrast presentation students see on social media. Even minor changes, such as enclosing reading passages and texts in boxes, made students less likely to quit. Text boxes provide a framed structure to help organize assignments and create more explicit expectations for students by separating readings from questions. Students benefit from this simple design because it is more in line with other forms of content they consume outside of school. This change especially helps Tier 1 students, who are much more optimistic about assignments when they can see that the text is manageable and easy to read.

Changing the length of assignments can also limit potential student Quit Points. Our goal is to use the minimum number of questions we need to see evidence of student learning. The longer an assignment, the higher the risk of Effort Rationing and reaching a Quit Point. Repetition may be an essential way of practicing new skills and content, but it doesn't have to be an important part of assignments. We prefer to break up repetitive tasks over the course of multiple days to make sure students provide authentic effort on each one. This strategy can significantly impact how students perceive recurring questions. Answering 30 similar math problems may result in fatigue and boredom, but solving a similar entry-level question on multiple assignments can reinforce optimism by making it easier for students to see the connection between previous and new learning. This way we present an experience that feels different but still accomplishes the same goals as in a more traditional classroom.

Visual cues are another easy way to build optimism for students beginning an assignment. Since Tier 1 Quit Points will occur at this time, we designed our optimism-building strategies with them in mind. Pairing images with text or providing the first operation of multi-step questions prevents students from assuming that the assignment is too challenging. The goal of these visual supports is to give students confidence that they can complete their tasks independently. Once they start, they will usually be able to take on more difficult challenges, thanks to the optimism they gain from the first part of the assignment. Every year, we try to learn from our students and make our visual presentation cleaner and more encouraging. They see we've adapted based on their feedback, and it demonstrates the student-driven culture we value.

We designed the feedback part of an assignment for students to complete with the assistance of peers or the teacher. Open-ended questions provide opportunities for students to improve their responses, either through a greater depth of knowledge or higher-level skills. Our goal is to strengthen the average quality of answers through teacher feedback and peer collaboration. We can gain a better understanding of what students' best work looks like when we focus on how they improved, rather than what they completed while Effort Rationing. This feedback can help shift students toward more engagement, which makes quitting less likely. The expectation helps reduce Quit Points because students don't feel that we're expecting a perfect answer on their first attempt, making them more likely to try and seek feedback for improvement.

We design feedback to be short and immediate. We may

ask students to paraphrase a response, give an example or analogy, compare, or relate something to previous learning and experiences. We offer the same feedback over again until the students can perform the task independently. Then we shift to a new focus and repeat the process to slowly build skills and knowledge over the course of the year. This process teaches our students the vocabulary necessary to improve collaboration. They are better equipped to work together because they learn to help each other by providing feedback that is similar to that given by the teacher. This culture of feedback and collaboration increases the support available to students by providing more options for assistance when they struggle in class. Many can avoid their Quit Points by turning to peers for help when they can't succeed on their own.

Not every student will be able to meet our expectations on every assignment. Sometimes the obstacles students face during the day overshadow our best attempts at structuring assignments to build optimism. Others may not have the stamina, or may not see enough task value in collaboration, and become disengaged during the feedback and growth part of the assignment. For these students, we provide opportunities for independent exploration to help them avoid quitting. Teachers can use this strategy as an intervention for those who struggle with the original goal of the assignment, or just as a change in routine. The goal, in this case, is not to show better learning, but to demonstrate any learning at all. If a student has reached a Quit Point, it is better to have learned *something* related to the lesson, than to focus on a narrow learning target, failing, and giving up.

TEACHER TAKEAWAY

The immediate takeaway to apply in your classroom is that you can incorporate tiering into any part of your class that requires support. Some educators may blueprint to ensure an appropriate balance between expectations and skills. Others may choose to restructure their lessons and assignments. Even attempting a small part of the tiered structure will improve your ability to avoid student Quit Points and will make differentiation easier. Below is our checklist of strategies and feedback for students of each tier, to help you in your own process.

Tier 1 Checklist	❏ Text paired with images
	❏ Give students step 1 of multi-step questions/problems
	❏ Reduce, reuse and recycle—simplify/limit questions, repeat key ideas/questions over multiple assignments, save completed work as background to new work
	❏ Have a summary question to address main goal of assignment
	❏ Share answer/ideas with a classmate
	❏ Paraphrase partner's ideas

Tier 2 Checklist	❏ Graphic organizers for new learning
	❏ Model responses
	❏ Emphasize comparisons and elaborations
	❏ Connect to outside/personal experience
	❏ Help a peer revise
	❏ Help focus partner's work to increase clarity

Tier 3 Checklist	❏ Provide analogies
	❏ Emphasis on creative freedom
	❏ Case studies and "Deep Dives"
	❏ Evaluating and ranking
	❏ Debate and defend
	❏ Peer support and coaching

Figure 4.4: When differentiating lessons, account for the skill levels and potential Quit Points of students. This checklist provides reminders for designing lessons and resources for students in different tiers.

Tiering	
Limited	❏ Teachers have standard assignments regardless of student skill level ❏ Teachers provide make-up work as remediation and extra credit as extension assignments ❏ Teachers use daily assignments to determine a grade
Progressing	❏ Teachers modify assignments to assist students who are struggling with learning goals ❏ Teachers assign projects that allow students to use various learning styles to demonstrate learning ❏ Teachers use daily assignments to determine ability levels
Advanced	❏ Teachers provide multiple assignments that reflect different goals and expectations depending on student skill level ❏ Teachers provide flexible time and choices to facilitate remediation or independent exploration ❏ Teachers use daily assignments to determine motivation levels and individual growth targets

Figure 4.5: Tiering Rubric

Blueprinting	
Limited	❏ Teachers use a standard assessment based on content alignment to standards ❏ Teachers rely on repetition in order to ensure daily assignments prepare students for assessments
Progressing	❏ Teachers use open-response questions on assessments to capture a wider range of student learning ❏ Teachers rely on rigor of daily assignments to prepare students for assessments
Advanced	❏ Teachers ensure assessments are balanced and designed to fit the needs and strengths of all learners ❏ Teachers use daily assignments to develop content skills that will support higher achievement on assessments

Figure 4.6: Blueprinting Rubric

Lesson Planning	
Limited	❏ Teachers design lessons to fill class time ❏ Teachers plan lessons using school-provided resources
Progressing	❏ Teachers design lessons with clear learning targets and include active learning activities ❏ Teachers plan lessons using additional resources to supplement district resources
Advanced	❏ Teachers design lessons to build optimism, provide time for feedback, and facilitate independent exploration ❏ Teachers plan lessons in which students are encouraged to discover and use resources that connect their interests to the curriculum

Figure 4.7: Lesson Planning Rubric

Resource Design	
Limited	❏ Teachers never modify resources before distributing to students ❏ Teachers avoid assigning questions that don't come with an answer key
Progressing	❏ Teachers edit resources to ensure they provide clear opportunities to demonstrate learning ❏ Teachers make sure every assignment has clear directions on how to show high-quality work
Advanced	❏ Teachers make sure that every assignment is presented in a student-friendly format ❏ Teachers make sure every assignment provides opportunities to give feedback to students

Figure 4.8: Resource Design Rubric

CHAPTER 5

ENRICHING ASSESSMENT: AVOID THE MINEFIELD OF GRADING QUIT POINT

Improve formative assessment and feedback through attainable goals

> "Learning happens in the minds and souls,
> not in the databases of multiple-choice tests."
> −SIR KEN ROBINSON

THERE IS ONE word that is responsible for most teacher stress: grading. Teachers are told to be fair and objective, but the growing stack of papers on their desks is a constant reminder of the work that awaits them. When teachers are working at home in the evenings and on weekends, they're not busy planning lessons; they're grading. Early in their careers, teachers usually resort to grading the way their childhood teachers graded them. Once comfortable with their system, they are often reluctant to change their approach. They worry that new ideas or strategies will send their workload spiraling out of control. For these reasons, teachers fail to recognize the minefield of Quit Points caused by traditional grading.

We commonly hear questions about grading when discussing Quit Point strategies. Teachers often agree with many aspects of our approach to learning, but struggle to fit the concepts into their established grading model. If the teacher focuses on preventing Quit Points, providing practice opportunities for growth, and allowing student exploration, those concepts do not fit neatly into traditional grading systems which are designed to plug in numbers per assignment and

> Grades are as much a measure of a student's ability and willingness to game the system as they are an accurate measure of learning.

spit out a final grade. Unfortunately, that method ignores the potential for irrational student behavior and the variables that impact effort—and the fact that those things can adversely affect student learning. Focusing on the numbers instead of reducing the quitting can inadvertently create more opportunities for students to quit.

Distractions occur because teachers are over-reliant on points and grades to communicate the importance of assignments. Students learn what their teachers value based on how many points assignments are worth and whether they will impact their final grades. The wide variety of point values teachers award to types of work can distract students from maintaining Regular Productive Effort. Any confusion about the relative importance of various activities can lead to quitting. If students can't see how their task is an essential part of class goals, it becomes more likely for them to prioritize other activities, such as social media, or procrastinate and Effort Ration until they reach the "important" part of the lesson.

A grade on an assignment is supposed to reflect understanding based on authentic student effort, but that is rarely the case. Students don't give 100 percent on every assignment. Students can complete many of those assignments with a fraction of their full effort, and even if they tried to maintain maximum performance, few students could sustain it for an entire day of classes. This reality makes it easy for teachers to accidentally permit students to quit. Traditional grading limits feedback to a score or percentage that approximates the level of learning. Students use these scores to justify quitting. When an assignment is only worth five points compared to the usual 20, the student's thought process is to Effort Ration because "the assignment is less important." An upcoming test worth 100 points might cause some students to quit because they "never get higher than a C on tests."

Grades are as much a measure of a student's ability and willingness to game the system as they are an accurate measure of learning. To resolve these obstacles, we started to focus on what was truly necessary for assessing student learning. What we wanted was better information than what we had—columns of numbers in a grade book or points per assignment. We needed assessment, not grades. Assessment focuses on information, feedback, and reflection. So, we designed assignments that provide both the teacher and student with information about the learning that has taken place. We share focused and meaningful feedback with the student to encourage reflection and growth instead of completion. Learning should be a collaborative process, and assessment must be a collaborative communication tool between the teacher and student. To improve our communication and better impact Quit Points, we ditched the numbers and focused on better information and focused feedback.

The first thing we needed to understand was when a student reached a Quit Point during an assignment. The learning students show before a Quit Point is always a better reflection of what they can do than what they demonstrate after. It is more effective to reassess students at a time when they are authentically engaged, instead of wasting energy scoring the responses that come after they quit. The problem is, we can never be sure if poor answers are due to a need for further learning or if they happen because the students stopped showing their knowledge after they quit. This qualitative difference between student responses that came from real effort compared to those that occurred after the Quit Point made us realize that focusing only on right answers and completion was completely incorrect. As soon as we changed our approach, we gained a better picture of our students' content knowledge, skills, and depth of understanding.

We realized that changing our approach to assessment could also allow us to communicate more about learning than a number or letter grade. A grade alone doesn't explain areas of strengths, what can be improved, and how to show growth. Also, any valuable feedback is usually ignored when students see a grade. We wanted to create a conversation about how to grow as learners. To improve our communication with students, we established a new procedure for providing focused feedback. This change transformed our conversations about learning and made a significant positive impact on student Quit Points.

FORMATIVE ASSESSMENT

Placing a heavy emphasis on grades distracts students from any other information teachers try to communicate. What should be the beginning of a meaningful interaction that facilitates learning instead funnels all parties on to the next activity. The teacher tracks the score on the assignment instead of expecting improvement. The students see their grades and focus on the next opportunity to earn points, so they can maintain or improve their achievements. The grade itself is the signal that quitting is OK, and the opportunity for learning is over for that activity.

Our goals for formative assessment are much closer to that of coaches and music teachers. We want to observe students in the process of working, instead of when they are "done." This strategy allows us to use our assessment to help them increase the effort and energy they dedicate to learning. Students who are still in the process of working can take on instruction and use it to improve their understanding of what they need to do. Our feedback changed from a number to information students could use to improve immediately.

Coaches and directors do not wait several days to communicate their evaluation to their players or performers. And yet that's what teachers do all the time. Coaches and directors continually assess musicians and athletes and give focused feedback during practices. Pitchers may work on their release, basketball players may focus on their defensive footwork, and musicians may be directed to pay careful attention to their breathing. Assigning a grade to each player in these examples would be silly because coaches know their players are not yet ready to perform to their full abilities. Instead, they help the players pay more attention to the elements of the game that could lead to significant impact on the field. To stress this aspect, we use the term "practice" to describe regular formative assessment. We want to observe students in action, evaluate their learning at the moment, and direct their focus toward the area of greatest need. Since they use our feedback to improve their performance, this means students begin to seek out more assessment of their performance in class. We started to use this assessment as a strategy to avoid Quit Points.

To use feedback to nudge students toward more engaged effort, we organized our assessment into three areas: content, skills, and depth. A feedback score of C, S, or D provides the students with more information than a numerical score. If a student sees a 64 percent on a paper, it doesn't necessarily communicate what they need to do to improve. This uncertainty leads to most students quitting instead of reading any comments or correction their teacher included. Before we shifted our feedback, we saw many students throwing their work in the trash instead of reading the comments we wrote. Now we use the "scores" of C, S, or D to provide students with a clear target for improvement, so they can sustain their effort instead of quitting.

> Rather than limiting ourselves to the results of quizzes and tests, we used formative practice work to make every assignment a chance to assess student learning. Since we were observing student work in real time, we had a better understanding of what work occurred before and after they reached a Quit Point.

We approach content, skills, and depth as a continuum rather than an average score. All students begin by learning the content for each unit. Once they can show understanding of that material, they start focusing on skills, such as communicating a more extensive range of knowledge. Finally, we expect those who show a firm grasp of content and skills to work toward higher-level thinking and greater depth of understanding. Students move along the continuum at different rates. Some may be able to show content mastery in only a few assignments, while others need to maintain their content focus for almost the entire unit. Since we don't provide numerical scores or letter grades, our students can work at a personalized pace instead of trying to keep a strict assignment schedule. This strategy allows us to use multiple assignments over the course of a unit to evaluate the learning of each student differently, since we track progress on the continuum instead of via columns of scores on assignments. This system helps prevent quitting, because at-risk students aren't weighed down by low scores that make higher achievement impossible. Those at the top of the continuum also quit less because their strong performance allows them to focus on independent learning and projects instead of activities they might perceive as busywork.

As we refined our efforts toward focused feedback, every day became an opportunity to better understand the depth of our students' learning. Rather than limiting ourselves to the results of quizzes and tests, we used formative practice work to make every assignment a chance to assess student learning. Since we were observing student work in real time, we had a better understanding of what work occurred before and after they reached a Quit Point. We also increased our ability to intervene and adjust things when unpredictable or irrational student behaviors prevented us from achieving our original lesson goals. We could use feedback to emphasize gaps in content, such as a lack of vocabulary in responses, or when we recognized symptoms of quitting, like procrastination or distraction. This approach kept the attention of the students on their academic goals instead of undesirable classroom conduct that occurred after their Quit Points. As a result, our formative assessment could improve our ability to teach and reduce the students' tendency to quit.

CONTENT

When we assess for content, we focus on main ideas, vocabulary, and whether students can provide examples. In humanities classrooms, this could mean being able to explain why a war started or the theme of a text. In STEM classrooms, this could be knowing that you need to combine like terms or test a hypothesis. We begin by ensuring that all students understand the main ideas from our unit. As they become more fluent in explaining those main ideas, we introduce and connect new vocabulary. Finally, once our students can use content-specific vocabulary, we ask them to provide examples from class as support and evidence of their learning.

This progression increases our awareness of where every individual is in the learning process. It directs our pacing through the unit and provides information to help avoid Quit Points as students study new material. Tier 1 students in particular can quickly become overwhelmed when they believe the expectation is to memorize disconnected facts. Communicating feedback to these students through terms like main ideas, vocabulary, and examples helps to provide attainable goals when they might otherwise be frustrated by their lack of learning. We ask students to explain what they know under the broad categories that make up content, to keep the focus on their existing knowledge instead of what they don't understand. This approach helps maintain a more optimistic mindset about learning and keeps students from reaching a Quit Point.

When students are independently capable of showing their content understanding, we consider them to have mastered their learning objectives. This assessment means they begin to communicate their learning with appropriate vocabulary and examples before they receive feedback. Also, students who have mastered their content learning will be able to assist their peers and provide additional support, parallel to what we give as teachers. We assess their level of independent and peer interaction and know which students can help assist their peers in avoiding Quit Points. Pairing a student who has a greater ability to demonstrate independent learning with a student who is more likely to quit can be a key intervention. They can articulate ideas in a more student-friendly manner, and make learning seem less stressful.

Once we see this level of mastery, we can confidently change the focus to the next level of feedback: skills.

SKILLS

Students who need skills feedback are the ones whose work doesn't consistently reflect their content learning. Their answers may be incomplete, disorganized, or lacking in clarity. When focusing on skills, we work to improve their ability to organize and communicate a broader range of learning. These expectations may include the ability to group common terms, explain cause and effect relationships, or even structure their understanding in a well-crafted essay. While these skills may extend beyond the reach of some students, feeling confident about their content knowledge makes it more likely they will persevere instead of quitting while working toward these goals.

Once students learn to share more of what they know, they are ready to show a more comprehensive understanding of their learning by practicing higher-level thinking skills and greater depth of knowledge. Students with skills mastery are those who demonstrate high-level skills before receiving feedback, and who can support their peers. They should be able to not only organize their learning, but also clarify class goals for their classmates. For example, if a student can facilitate a discussion around the takeaway from a unit, he or she is ready for a more complex and personal experience. Shifting focus toward greater depth is necessary to help those students avoid Effort Rationing on skills-based learning.

Once students reach this level, they are ready for the next level of feedback: depth.

DEPTH

To be able to focus our highest-skilled students on appropriate growth targets and ensure more frequent authentic engagement, we assess and provide feedback to students based on their depth and complexity of learning. At this point, students should be able to link themes across units, relate learning to personal experiences, and evaluate various arguments or ideas. Due to their mastery of both content and skills, we encourage students who receive depth feedback to explore areas of specific interest. This strategy supports Tier 3 students' need for independence. The emphasis changes from doing more to doing "better." Our depth feedback becomes the guideline for what students should be able to achieve when they try to do better. Just rehashing the same standards over again makes quitting more likely. We need to make it more exciting.

These students can answer recall and memory questions

so easily that we must focus on higher-complexity questions to keep them engaged. Repetitive, low-level tasks are tedious and seem like busywork, which leads these students to reach a Quit Point. It is much more effective to ask them to personalize their learning. We assess students who can personalize learning based on their abilities to reflect on their knowledge. These are the students who teach us. We may not know that a Disney movie shares a theme with Thoreau's *Civil Disobedience,* or that a video game demonstrates the main ideas of a topic we've been learning about—but students can use that connection to enhance their learning. At other times, we may learn that a student's struggles relate to what we want to learn as a class. Communicating these experiences and trying to think about school in such a personal way shows students' complex mastery of learning. It also reduces the likelihood of quitting because students have more freedom to bring their interests into the classroom.

Extension opportunities do not require the same degree of focused remediation as content and skills feedback. Once students have mastered complex learning expectations, with the help of guided feedback for depth, they can explore and connect ideas that most peers, and even teachers, might not understand at first. At this point, the role of the teacher is to get out of their way. These students can wander down the rabbit hole of their choosing, and still find their way home. What they bring back, such as the role of refrigerated train cars during industrialization, the parallels between a Batman villain and the French Revolution, or an app like Pokémon that lets them hunt for flora and fauna, has the potential to enrich everyone's learning.

RETHINKING ASSESSMENT SOUNDS GREAT, BUT I STILL HAVE TO ASSIGN A GRADE LIKE ANY OTHER TEACHER

The most common pushback from colleagues about our assessment changes has been that they aren't sure how to use our strategies to assign traditional grades. Like most teachers, we are required to enter final grades for each student. We send them out to students and parents with nothing more than generic comments such as, "Pleasure to have in class" or "Distracts students around him/her." But what does a grade or comment of "C+" and "Regularly on task" mean? How is a student supposed to improve on that?

Instead of standard grades, we model our final grading system on mastery and standards-based grading systems. Many schools openly embrace these new approaches to grading, which emphasize the demonstration of learning rather than a traditional approach. Some educators even go as far as getting rid of grades entirely, as shown by the community of "Teachers Throwing Out Grades." We, however, are expected to give a final score at the end of the term, and don't have the option of throwing grades out completely. Instead, we use our feedback progression, along with mastery assessment, to determine the final score for each student. We use summative assessments to establish a baseline level of mastery and daily formative practice work to determine when students are ready for this final assessment. Our students' personalized learning experiences allow us to determine growth and learning beyond the narrow confines of the standard. Their grades also reflect the journey and exploration that was part of the process. The final grade isn't a simple average based on their work, but an aggregation of their experiences.

We expect learning to be a process. Students should not fear punitive grades for the growing pains that are merely part of that process. But by focusing on learning that occurs before the Quit Point, teachers can gather more and better information about student learning. That allows educators to give focused feedback that doesn't penalize mistakes, but provides each learner with the opportunity to improve. The worlds of sports, arts, and business do not rely on a single grade as a measure of an individual's performance, and it's time more teachers embraced meaningful assessment. We do not need to accept a grading system just because "that's the way it's always been done." Courageous educators have the power to make the change—and it starts with the way we're assessing our students, and how we're treating the process of learning.

TEACHER TAKEAWAY

Assessment is a critical element of effective teaching and learning, and we need to address it to positively impact student Quit Point. The first step an educator should take is to differentiate between assessment and grading. Focus on the informative nature of assessment rather than the punitive nature of grading. Assessment should provide educators and students with information about learning so that both sides can communicate and collaborate toward improvement. This strategy is the starting point for providing meaningful feedback, which allows students to improve upon their prior learning. Once teachers assign a grade in a traditional system, students view the process as complete, and stop seeking improvement. Offering simple, focused feedback such as C, S, and D makes it less likely that students will quit because they understand what they can do to improve.

As teachers focus more on the process of assessment and less on the result of grading, they will strengthen the optimism and task value of their students, and reduce their likelihood of reaching Quit Points.

Feedback		
Limited	❑ Teachers provide feedback via letter grades and numerical scores ❑ Teachers provide feedback to students after the assignment has been turned in ❑ Teachers provide feedback to explain the rationale behind the score or grade	
Progressing	❑ Teachers provide suggestions for improvement along with a letter grade or score ❑ Teachers provide feedback in a timely manner so improvements can be made on future assignments ❑ Teachers give feedback that is focused on students who are struggling	
Advanced	❑ Teachers provide feedback based on students' individual growth targets ❑ Teachers offer feedback while students are working on the assignment so they can improve upon their work in the moment ❑ Teachers use focused feedback to help all students reach deeper levels of understanding	

Figure 5.1: Feedback Rubric

Grading		
Limited	❑ Teachers grade for completion ❑ Teachers give grades to show whether students turn in assignments	
Progressing	❑ Teachers assign grades based on the average level of learning demonstrated by students ❑ Teachers give grades to show whether students are achieving learning targets	
Advanced	❑ Teachers assign grades based on mastery of learning ❑ Teachers give grades that reflect what students need to do to achieve learning objectives	

Figure 5.2: Grading Rubric

CHAPTER 6

EMPOWERING STUDENTS THROUGH CLIMATE AND CULTURE

Incorporate teams, leaders, and games to prevent quitting

"Give the children an opportunity to make
a garden. Let them grow what they will.
It matters less that they grow good plants
than that they try for themselves."
—LIBERTY HYDE BAILEY

THE TEACHER ORGANIZES handouts as students walk into the room. They take their seats as the bell rings. The teacher introduces the lesson while passing out papers, and sees a student playing a video game on his phone. "Put your phone away, Devin," the teacher says expectedly. Unfortunately, Devin chooses to ignore the request. The teacher walks over and repeats the directive while standing next to the student. Still, there is no response. At this point, the entire class is watching in hushed anticipation. Moments like this turn into power struggles, and the conflict is bound to overshadow the learning goals for the day. Devin will now have to overcome a Quit Point before learning anything, and if the teacher isn't careful, many more students may also quit due to the stressful climate in the classroom.

Avoiding these scenarios is one of the toughest responsibilities educators face. Teachers must know how to de-escalate potential power struggles, communicate clear expectations, and build positive relationships with students. Even when the teacher has done everything possible to set a positive classroom climate, conflicts arise because children's behavior is unpredictable. Since students often struggle to regulate their actions, the teacher feels a responsibility to show who's in charge. While that seems like

> By distributing responsibility to all parties, we stopped trying to win power struggles and learned that student leadership could be as important as teacher action in avoiding Quit Points.

the logical response for an adult in a position of authority, the constant attempts to maintain control can make the culture worse. The question is: Could classroom culture improve if the adults worked to empower their students?

In some schools, teachers expect kindergarteners to lead a parent-teacher conference. They share what they have learned and facilitate conversation between their parents and teachers. The adults know the student is capable of the responsibility and are there to guide and support the child if there is a problem. This process distributes responsibility to all parties involved, so the teacher doesn't have to shoulder the burden alone. This example stands in stark contrast to the scenario explained in the opening paragraph. Most teachers' evaluations use adult actions to determine the success of their lessons. But the process needs to recognize student behaviors instead. What if all teachers learned to share responsibility for classroom climate and expectations? If kindergarten students can lead conferences, then all students should be able to show ownership of their learning. Would greater student autonomy help prevent more Quit Points than the teacher could prevent alone?

We tested this hypothesis by creating a program for student ownership—and it quickly evolved into a comprehensive, student-driven classroom environment. Empowered student leaders formed teams and shaped the climate and culture of the classroom. They stopped passively entering class and waiting for the teacher to take action. Before the bell even had a chance to ring, they hurried to collaborate or compete with their peers. Before we needed to intervene, we noticed both leaders and teammates helping to prevent their peers from quitting. Our experiment was a resounding success. By distributing responsibility to all parties, we stopped trying to win power struggles and learned that student leadership could be as important as teacher action in avoiding Quit Points. We had changed the culture and climate—and we were all reaping the benefits.

STUDENT TEAMS AND LEADERS

The start of our team organization system was an accidental byproduct of our learning to teach in a technology-facilitated classroom. Each student used a Chromebook as an educational resource daily. We were among the first teachers in the district to have this level of access, so most of the students were uncomfortable with the new tools. Fortunately, each class had a few students who were confident enough with computers that they could help us troubleshoot, and support peers who were interacting with a computer for the first time. Our unofficial student technology experts meant that we could walk the room at the start of the period to make sure everyone could log in and begin the lesson. Without the help of these informal student leaders, we would have taken much longer to start class each day.

We decided to go even further and expand the role of the leaders to see if we could gain even more benefits.

Leaders needed to feel empowered to best represent their peers. We didn't want to cause Quit Points due to embarrassment from peers calling them "teacher's pets." Our technology helpers managed to avoid those types of accusations because their role was to be experts and peer ambassadors.

They often told us how to solve problems and intervened on behalf of introverted students who were hesitant to speak up. Similarly, our formal class leaders needed to represent the students, not the teacher. To achieve this, we had to take a risk. We gave our students the power to choose their leaders—even if it meant they selected individuals we were concerned about empowering.

We were pleasantly surprised with how well the strategy worked. Student control over the selection of leaders resulted in spontaneous debates and elections. The students elected were eager to take on significant leadership roles and provide support to help prevent their peers from quitting.

Team formation was also student-led. We didn't worry about friends being together, whether there was a balance of ability levels, or any of the other concerns stressed in teacher education classes. What mattered was that students felt a sense of belonging to the team. We also wanted the leaders, as team representatives, to take responsibility for the success of the group. Dividing friends, meticulously creating balanced groups, and scripting interactions can be productive for a lesson, but will do little to empower the class or your students. In our experience, "group work" often resulted in Effort Rationing and quitting. Students complained about the peers in their group or their assigned roles. The best students usually detested group work because they knew the burden would fall on their shoulders. We did not want our classroom teams to resemble those traditional models for organizing students. The goal was to unlock their potential rather than limiting them through assigned roles. In the end, groups of three to 10 students formed organically, based entirely on their choices.

To guide the students, we started with two simple expectations about leaders and teams. First, team members should always go to a peer before asking the teacher any non-academic question. This strategy completely transformed our role, because the responsibility for basic procedures and directions shifted to the students. We no longer answered the same procedural questions over and over during the lesson because the teams learned to regulate themselves.

Second, leaders needed to share the positive achievements of their teams. This approach changed the vocabulary students used to describe their success from "I" to "we." The initial results from this experiment were encouraging.

The classroom climate changed significantly, thanks to the student leaders and teams. The teacher no longer struggled to maintain control because the students took on that responsibility. The emphasis of our role shifted from just reciting procedures… to taking part in academic reinforcement. This change also reduced the likelihood of confrontations and power struggles. Students displayed less initial quitting, like in the example of Devin on his cell phone, because they didn't want to disappoint their self-selected leaders. Finally, more introverted and successful students showed more initiative to support their peers and help their team.

It didn't take us long to decide to further explore the success of the team dynamic.

DAILY ACTION GOALS

We found that some students had a natural inclination for leadership. Others had a higher learning curve before they could be effective. Regardless of how they functioned as individuals, all students needed a nudge to function better as a team. The traditional approach would be to use specific classroom rules to communicate our expectations for their behavior. The problem with that approach was that it would undermine the goal of empowering the students. Providing a list of rules everyone was supposed to follow would shift the ownership and responsibility back to the teacher. We would be right back where we started, with a more traditional power structure based on the teacher's ability to maintain control. It would bring back all the Quit Points that students avoided through their teams and leaders. To keep the focus on student autonomy, we decided to frame our daily action goals as choices rather than rules.

Choices, as opposed to rules, are scaffolds that help students understand what they can do to be more effective in class. The goal is like giving students the first step in a multi-step math equation. It points them in the right direction. If students don't make a choice, it demonstrates that they're past their Quit Point, and not interested in classroom goals at that moment. But giving them the choice means that the teacher doesn't have to correct any behavior. The action goals allow students to show they want to move toward engagement. Ultimately, the choice belongs to the students, and they maintain ownership over their classroom conduct.

We made posters that shared these daily action goals with the students so they could understand how their actions displayed their engagement. They could complete any first-level choice in mere seconds. There were easy ways to determine whether students were moving toward classroom goals or if they were stuck in their Quit Point. To show they were ready to learn, team members could choose to find a seat, put their phones down or away, and try the first steps of the assignment. Leaders' choices included checking that everyone on their team knew what they were supposed to do or getting out of their seat to help a peer. Any of these actions moved students toward greater productivity without much effort. The posters guided students to choices that were more effective for learning, while not infringing on the autonomy of those who regularly showed higher levels of engagement on their own.

To continually stress student ownership, we made a concerted effort not to treat the daily action goals as expectations. Some leaders chose to ignore all the options offered because they had alternative ways of taking responsibility. One student liked to complete all her assignments early as homework, then sit in a circle with her team and serve as a tutor to help everyone else understand the lesson. She regularly asked for feedback at the start of class to make sure she understood the assignment, and then spent the rest of the period supporting her team. We didn't try to convince her to make more choices based on the daily action goals. Instead, we praised her initiative in taking responsibility for her group. She was so effective that several other leaders modeled their structures after her system. Others preferred to follow the suggested choices to improve their productivity. In each instance, we watched team spirit and the actions of the leader reduce the occurrence of quitting.

Whether through procrastination, avoidance, or distraction, quitting manifests in academic non-action. Distracted students show personal behaviors such as talking instead of engaging in classroom goals. Procrastinators try to do as little as possible until the last moment. Daily action goals highlight student choices as the determining factor for success in the classroom. They can choose to shift into a more active learning state with minimal effort and maintain a baseline level of engagement that makes quitting less likely. Our role as teachers isn't to make choices for students. We merely support and assist them in taking ownership of their learning.

As teams and leaders became comfortable with the basic options in the daily action goals, we recognized the need to increase the ways that students could become highly effective. The first choices shared ways for students to show that they were ready for engagement. The goal of the next level was to give examples of actions that would show students were authentically engaged and interested in learning. We wanted to shift students from Effort Rationing to high levels of effort. Team members could check in with a peer, improve an answer, or help a classmate. Leaders could communicate greater engagement by sharing team achievements or discussing effective strategies with other leaders. These action goals were still just choices, and leaders sometimes found other ways to be highly

> The opening moments of a lesson provide teachers with an opportunity to engage students and build momentum. So often, teachers overlook this chance in favor of completing menial tasks like attendance, handouts, or a "bell ringer" assignment.

engaged. One leader would use feedback from his group to call a "timeout" during class when the team needed additional support. They would then call the teacher for small-group instruction based on their specific learning needs. These student choices showed commitment to improvement and responsibility for their learning. Having the autonomy to make decisions that best impacted their work on a given day helped to prevent Quit Points that would otherwise be present in a teacher-controlled class.

The introduction of daily action goals successfully supported leaders who needed help knowing how to take responsibility for the success of their teams. The choices also provided an easy tool to help students move away from quitting and Effort Rationing. The new student-driven classroom climate resulted in fewer conflicts and power struggles. We also saw higher levels of engagement. We learned inspiring lessons from the students who took full control and shaped the identity and success of teams. Many leaders, like in the examples listed above, provided new insights into how students preferred to learn and support each other. The most significant impact was on how our lessons started. Most classes began before the bell, because the new structure helped everyone start as they came into the room. Students no longer needed to wait on us for directions because their teams made sure everyone knew what to do. This success prompted us to entrust the responsibility for starting the class to team leaders. It was the start of what we called "Challenge Time."

TEAM CHALLENGES

The opening moments of a lesson provide teachers with an opportunity to engage students and build momentum. So often, teachers overlook this chance in favor of completing menial tasks like attendance, handouts, or a "bell ringer" assignment. Meanwhile, students enter with so many other mental distractions that they don't perceive the opening moments of class as important. The problem with trying to cram as much as possible into a bell-to-bell window is that it does not create a culture in which students feel empowered. Our experiences with teams and student leaders proved that autonomy was more important than time management in preventing many of the Quit Points that gridlocked learning. And since the team structure was already in place and so successful, it was a logical progression to use that foundation to begin lessons through team challenges.

We structure challenges to promote a positive attitude while students are in our classes. We focus on simple strategies that build optimism and ease social interactions to start each lesson with everyone feeling confident about his or her ability to learn. Some students reach a Quit Point merely because they can't answer the bell ringer question or can't connect to the lesson "hook." Team challenges limit that immediate quitting because everyone can achieve them, regardless of academic strengths. We don't even need to restrict activities to those that are explicitly content-related. Any opportunity for students to show creativity, communication, and collaboration helps them begin class with momentum. The teacher's role is simply to encourage leaders to take ownership over the learning process.

We used our team structure to create fun challenges. This approach built enthusiasm and helped remind students that learning is a collaborative process, which includes experimentation and mistakes. Since we didn't emphasize content, we focused on student interests and activities that encouraged teamwork. We found that creating simple goals was essential for maximizing the potential of challenges, and we avoided giving directions that limit students' creative impulses. This strategy freed them to go above and beyond to succeed on the task. How the group worked to meet that goal was up to them. When a challenge is successful in encouraging enthusiasm, it can result in entire teams starting class without approaching any Quit Points.

One memorable challenge had multiple steps for the team to complete within a short time. The entire task was impossible to achieve individually, so the leaders launched into action, delegating various parts to team members. The students seized full responsibility for helping their teams compete. One step required a member to sing aloud the song "Happy" by Pharrell Williams. Suddenly, one of the quietest kids in the room started belting out the lyrics at full volume. He wanted to win the competition with his team and was not about to lose because of a song. His team won, the class had a blast, and his group was empowered to work together to overcome their obstacles. Not having to worry about asserting our authority allowed us to unlock a genuine moment of collaboration and student ownership. This short challenge set a positive tone for the entire day's worth of learning because we made it fun.

The simplest way to make the challenges enjoyable is to tap

into student interests. Recognizing what they do for fun outside of class can quickly lead to new ideas. Elementary classrooms take dancing "brain breaks," and preschoolers learn to "shake the sillies out" to refocus. At the high school level, singing and dancing can also be a great way to engage students creatively. In our modern technological age, playing video games or using student devices can also open greater participation and teamwork in a realm in which they already feel comfortable. Once again, if the goal is momentum toward learning rather than content, the team challenge can be anything. While teacher blogs are full of complaints about the latest disruption-causing fads (fidget spinners, bottle flipping, cell phone games), we embrace those student interests to spur engagement. By showing our appreciation for these activities, we also limit the chances of conflict that can lead to quitting. Providing an outlet for the things students enjoy doing can help prevent frustration—for all of us.

One student-interest-themed challenge rewarded teams for videos of the most consecutive bottle flips, best dabs, and high scores on popular video games. The catch of this challenge was that the entire group needed to complete the day's assignment, and have it reviewed by the teacher before making any videos. We knew these activities tapped into student interests and hoped they would lead to higher engagement. The students worked diligently for a chance to share their skills. One team that usually Effort Rationed jumped at the opportunity to show off their non-academic abilities, sustained full effort throughout the class, and collaborated to make sure that all members demonstrated their learning to the teacher. This activity reduced the level of quitting by merely incorporating students' passions into the lesson.

A final guideline for using challenges is to recognize the efforts and successes of the teams. When a group is showing high levels of participation and collaboration, we like to honor their commitment to success. First, this provides a shot of encouragement to many students who rarely, if ever, receive positive feedback concerning their schoolwork. Beginning a lesson with words of encouragement and praise, even on non-academic activities, may be the catalyst that pushes students to avoid quitting altogether. Recognizing students for any positive effort in class helps reinforce the habits that lead to academic achievement.

For teachers looking to replace stale bell ringers with team challenges, here are three goals to keep in mind:

- Keep it fun

- Tap into student interests

- Recognize effort

If the objective is to begin a lesson with excitement, then devoting a few minutes to an activity that encourages student teams to collaborate and own their learning is a worthy investment. It just might be the difference between students who sustain effort and those who are quick to quit.

GAMIFICATION

Our success with incorporating fun and enthusiasm through challenges inspired the final step of our team structure.

Turning challenge time into a game allowed us to emphasize play and creativity, while simultaneously building content connections to team activities. But the initial goal of creating a climate and culture that empowered students wasn't enough. We quickly realized that we could be even more ambitious and incorporate their interests in online gaming and competition with friends. Student ownership of the classroom wasn't just an achievement; it was an artificial limitation. What if there was a way for them to show leadership over more than just their team? What if they had a chance to rule their own country, or even the world?

The gamification of our classroom quickly evolved into a year-long adventure. Educators have used this concept for some time, and it often centers around a reward structure that recognizes student achievement with badges or medals. Other examples include content simulations that resemble games. A famous example is the assembly line. Students play the role of workers while the teacher replicates the factory experience by capriciously hiring and firing.

Post-it notes describing injuries are attached to limbs, and prevent students from using those limbs during the rest of the activity. This process does not support student autonomy, however, because the goal is to reach and then debrief a result as a learning tool. The students are supposed to learn how difficult factory work was during the Industrial Revolution, but the simulation is so fun that students often remember their enjoyment more than the intended learning target. While there is value in this approach, it still fails to align with our objective of a student-driven classroom. It also fails to account for obstacles that could lead to quitting. If students don't connect with the limited goals of the activity, they may Effort Ration, or refuse to participate entirely.

We wanted to create a world within our class where the students were in control and weren't limited in potential outcomes. History has proven to be an inspiration for many films and games. Hollywood blockbusters like *Dunkirk* and games like Assassin's Creed show that people enjoy exploring and examining events of the past. Some appreciate the chance to learn more about the people and places that shaped our civilization. Others may imagine what they would do if they were in the situations they see on the screen. Many people even dress up and role-play characters from their favorite franchises. Historical entertainment provides a background that all viewers and players can use to interact with the content and each other. As social studies teachers, blending our team challenges with historical events offered the same opportunity to provide a backdrop that encouraged interactions between students and content.

As we pursued that goal, we decided to animate important class themes as parts of a much longer game. For instance, the teams became fully functioning businesses during the Industrial Revolution. The leader played the role of the factory owner and delegated responsibilities throughout the group as they raced to draw trains in an assembly line system. We "paid" the team leaders based on the number of trains completed, and then the leaders compensated individual members for their work. They also hired and fired workers as needed to increase profits and maintain optimal efficiency. As the owners, they could choose to invest their team's money into "cheat codes" that gave an advantage over their class competition, or in other high-performing groups through a stock market. Meanwhile, team members struggled to keep up with the increasing demand for trains. They were controlling how they dealt with obstacles, just like they would if they were reading a choose-your-own-adventure book.

The game was most successful when students responded with creativity rather than quitting during frustrating situations. An incompetent and cruel boss is enough for anyone to reach a Quit Point, whether in real life or in a classroom activity. Instead of causing disengagement in the context of the game, this obstacle led to the formation of labor unions, strikes, and even a full-blown Marxist revolution. We empowered students to shape their teams and build a world of their preference. Each choice they made to solve obstacles created new opportunities and challenges. One group decided to overthrow their "lazy" manager. They were so happy with the results of their choice that they sent emails to other teams, encouraging similar action. Other managers saw this as a threat and restricted cell phone and email access in their groups during factory time. Simulations limit students to the outcomes envisioned by the teacher. Our game harnessed the power of students' collective imaginations to create limitless possibilities.

As we progressed through the school year, factories became countries that developed unique cultures. They chose how to allocate their resources and even conquered other groups to increase their power. Sometimes students started a "global conflict" that played out during class. The game then helped facilitate students' understanding of the underlying causes of international hostilities. One student responded to the threat of global war by proposing solutions to avoid future conflicts. He generated an "international" email exchange with the intention of worldwide disarmament. Conversely, another group sought control of the entire class by devoting all their resources to military buildup. They also manipulated the class currency, which resulted in hyperinflation. The rest of the countries imposed a peace agreement that punished the antagonizing group, much like the Treaty of Versailles that ended World War I.

Student choices provided the context that allowed them to understand class content that related to the game. Previously, many of these historical events had been so outside student experience that they struggled to see any value in learning about them. Predictably, Quit Points arose more often during topics to which students did not connect. Gamification created a framework for students to create context, and this supported sustained effort through even the most challenging content standards. Instead of quitting, our students were engaged with and directing their own learning.

Teachers who want to maximize their instructional time can benefit by empowering students and incorporating play, rather than using bell-to-bell instruction. Giving students the ownership and authority to create a virtual world gave us the support we needed to make a significant impact in limiting quitting. We used the game to prevent Effort Rationing and non-participation, and we observed higher engagement during learning activities. Quitting decreased, and peak performances and sustained effort increased as the culture of the classroom shifted.

TEACHER TAKEAWAY

One way to prevent student Quit Points is by shaping the culture and classroom climate through student empowerment. Allowing students to self-select teams and leaders shows that they are capable of organizing groups without teacher oversight. They need to be able to make choices about how to manage themselves and show engagement in class. They may not always make the same decisions as the teacher would make, but they will feel that their role in class is meaningful and respond accordingly. Friendly competition and games can help reinforce a climate of student empowerment. Even short breaks that emphasize fun and play are enough to communicate that their interests are always at the forefront. When students have responsibility for their learning, they will step up and support the teacher in limiting Quit Points.

Student Teams	
Limited	❏ Teachers design group activities in which students have no opportunity to make choices ❏ Teachers assign rigid roles to students when they collaborate ❏ Teachers choose groups based on disciplinary concerns more than learning opportunities
Progressing	❏ Teachers are only comfortable with group activities which they directly supervise and assess ❏ Teachers create group activities in which student effort is lower than when they work individually ❏ Teachers spend more time redirecting groups than facilitating learning
Advanced	❏ Teachers encourage students to take full responsibility over their groups ❏ Teachers work with student leaders to help support all students and manage classroom expectations ❏ Teachers expect teams to initiate learning without directions

Figure 6.1: Student Teams Rubric

Daily Action Goals	
Limited	❏ Teachers assume full responsibility for student behavior through enforcement of classroom rules ❏ Teachers only draw attention to non-compliant behaviors
Progressing	❏ Teachers work with students to establish classroom expectations ❏ Teachers praise students who demonstrate positive behaviors
Advanced	❏ Teachers provide tools for students to self-regulate their behavior and learning habits ❏ Teachers allow students to create their own system for meeting learning goals and building a positive classroom climate

Figure 6.2: Daily Action Goals Rubric

CHAPTER 7

TRANSFERRING CULTURE TO LEARNING: USE TECHNOLOGY TO DODGE QUIT POINTS

Increase collaboration, participation, and student ownership through digital tools

"It's not the tools you have faith in. Tools are just tools—they work or they don't work. It's the people you have faith in or not."
—STEVE JOBS

SEVERAL YEARS AGO, we fully embraced the potential of technology and piloted a 1-to-1 model in our class. It was in these early stages of using 21st-century resources that we developed our understanding of Quit Point. We hoped to motivate the students to reach for higher levels of achievement if we provided them with new tools and resources. There are so many applications, programs, and devices designed for educational purposes, that the only barrier to meeting our goals was finding the right one. We attended an education technology conference with sessions that boasted "10 apps to transform your classroom," and vendors that promised their products would turn every student into a blossoming scholar. By using just a few of these tools, we could improve the learning experience. We believed our "digital native" students would respond to the changes with enthusiasm.

As we described in the introduction, we were naive to think using technology would be enough to end student apathy. It turned out that some of those new tools increased the frequency of quitting. Even helping everyone log in to their Chromebooks was a battle. It took weeks for us to overcome the tidal wave of Quit Points caused by students who struggled to access their device successfully. We concluded that we needed a plan to reduce technology-related quitting before we could expect to see any potential benefits. Some teachers view technology as the solution to obstacles, while others see it as the fundamental problem. In truth, it is neither the answer nor the problem. Technology is just a tool, and can harm or enhance the learning experience, depending on how you use it.

All digital tools and resources have the potential to add to the learning experience if teachers can limit Quit Points when they're introducing them. A good guideline is to consider how students use phones and tablets. It's common for children as young as age 1 to interact with these devices, and to watch songs and videos. Many toddlers can open applications and change videos on their own, after only a minute or two of learning. Some children are so interested in playing with these extremely accessible apps that they will spend

> No matter how well-designed the instructions are, if it takes students more than a minute to learn to use a new piece of technology, they are likely to reach a Quit Point rather than persevere.

hours staring at a screen unless a parent intervenes. Even the youngest kids can find this type of entertainment on their own. They don't need tutorials or extended experience to use a device.

Students want and expect any worthwhile technology to be as easy to use as the phones and tablets they have been using since early in life. The problem is, educational settings do not necessarily parallel this level of accessibility.

Teachers often begin using technology only after attending seminars or classes or viewing the types of tutorials that students avoid. They then present new tools with detailed directions, screenshots, or mini-video lessons to teach their students how to use them. But students shouldn't feel they must devote more time to learning about the technology than time spent on their class content goals. No matter how well-designed the instructions are, if it takes students more than a minute to learn to use a new piece of technology, they are likely to reach a Quit Point rather than persevere. They may quit just because they think it's too difficult to use, and as a result they don't accomplish any positive effects—which were the goals of the technology.

The potential rewards of paperless classrooms, virtual tours, and digital portfolios remain unrealized if students are too frustrated to persevere through tech-related barriers. In worst-case scenarios, technological hurdles can reduce students' optimism and feelings of self-efficacy to the point that they quit before giving their new tools a chance. Our mistake was introducing technology based on what we, as teachers, could do with it. However, it was vital to prioritize student needs if we wanted them to embrace new things. The most popular digital tools are created to help teachers ease the burden of grading, change reading resources, and organize classroom assignments. But the benefits go disproportionately to the teacher in all these examples. The experience of the student is rarely, if ever, addressed in educational technology. Some students may even perceive these tools as hoops to jump through for the sole purpose of making life easier for the teacher. When this occurs, the lack of task value for the student increases the likelihood of quitting.

Many students think about school as using paper and pencil. If all teachers do is digitize their assignments—while making them look the same way—their classes will not see the value in working with unfamiliar tools. Teachers assume that students prefer technology because they use mobile devices and computers for entertainment, but sharing pictures and watching videos isn't the same as reading and answering questions. Technology that aids education is more effective when it empowers students to do more than they could do with traditional resources. The key to avoiding Quit Points while incorporating more technology is to emphasize what the students want. If a new tool isn't easily accessible, valued by students, or a superior experience compared to the traditional classroom, then it will fail to improve the learning process.

NEW WAYS TO COLLABORATE

One of the most effective ways to use technology is for collaboration. Working together isn't always easy for students. Some lack the social skills needed to communicate effectively. Others fail to see the value in listening to peers if they already know the answer. Teachers try to support students by giving detailed directions and scripting roles to prevent these types of obstacles from interrupting learning, but these well-intentioned scaffolds create new problems. Teachers design instructions and routines to ensure student accountability and to monitor collaboration. Note-taking and sharing out to the class are some of these strategies. The emphasis on holding students accountable can distract from cooperative work, though, and sharing every answer makes learning slower and more repetitive. Fortunately, technology can eliminate these obstacles that lead to quitting.

Collaboration is easier when the entire group has access to the same information at the same time. Programs like Google Drive increase the accessibility of documents by allowing many people to view them at once. Sharing a document with a peer also takes less than a minute. Typical group roles, such as notetaker, become obsolete when the collective work is available to all parties all the time. This approach means that students don't need as many directions to know how to work together. They can decide their roles based on the requirements of the assignment. The ability to take more ownership of their responsibilities on a group document helps students avoid quitting. Instead of trying to role-play a task based on their teacher's expectations, they can engage in more authentic collaboration.

Not only is technological collaboration more effortless, it provides new opportunities to work together. When students digitally collaborate, they can incorporate a greater variety of resources. Multimedia documents, images, and videos are accessible through a simple click on their devices.

Sharing information is also less cumbersome when students don't need to be next to each other, or even talk at all, to work together. The ability to share without drawing the attention of everyone in the room is a tremendous development for introverted students. For example, we had a student who was mute. He never successfully worked with any of his peers before coming to our class. Any time teachers expected students to collaborate, he would reach an immediate Quit Point and isolate himself even further. When he learned that he could work with others without speaking, he became much more optimistic about his ability to collaborate. Through his writing on shared documents, he was able to contribute valuable insights based on his higher-level thinking skills. This development changed his peers' perception of him. They stopped thinking of him as "the weird, quiet kid," and started working with him.

Not only is technological collaboration more effortless, it provides new opportunities to work together. When students digitally collaborate, they can incorporate a greater variety of resources. Multimedia documents, images, and videos are accessible through a simple click on their devices. Students can discover, share, and discuss based on these types of files more easily than in a traditional paper-and-pencil classroom. When they don't have access to technology, they become dependent on the teacher and the quality of the copy machine if they want to use non-text resources.

Collaboration becomes a more productive experience when it involves using higher-quality, more accessible resources. Quit Points are less prevalent when color images, videos, and hyperlinks are included because those tools provide more engaging learning opportunities than paper. The emphasis on more visual images also parallels the types of entertainment students consume digitally. This approach gives them more opportunities to connect their interests to class goals.

Our digital adaptation of the jigsaw method of teaching is a good example of a collaborative technology experience. Groups worked on a shared document in which all members collected their research and thinking about a topic. They used a program called Scrible to annotate websites and highlight the main ideas. This program was linked to their Google Drive accounts, so they could search all their annotations without leaving their group document. Once all members had shared their research, they could read all the research, and discuss how it connected to their daily learning goal. They concluded by writing about their learning and citing evidence from all group members' research.

NEW WAYS TO PARTICIPATE

In most classrooms, when the teacher asks the class a question to determine whether the students understand the main idea of the lesson, the moment is a Quit Point for most of the class. This problem occurs because a minority of vocal students tends to dominate these opportunities for class participation. Those who don't know the answer or are too shy to speak in front of classmates can quit and wait for a vocal peer to draw the attention of the teacher. Even using more advanced questioning methods doesn't necessarily pry responses out of the quitting majority. Teachers can wait for more hands to rise, or use popsicle sticks to choose random students, but in the end, the class expects only three to five students to speak. This approach makes quitting the easiest choice.

Technology can make participation possible for all students, including introverts. We use an app called Pear Deck to collect and share class responses to questions. Rather than having to connect to a separate program, students click on a teacher-provided link that allows them to answer at their own pace. We display these responses and share them anonymously on the teacher's screen, allowing everyone to benefit from answers that provide the highest level of understanding. Students might not have shared many of these answers in a more traditional setting. We then discuss various submissions to assess how well the class understands the lesson. No student has to be afraid of embarrassment because participation is anonymous, and since the entire class is encouraged to respond, they can't expect three to five students to do all of the work.

Clicking a link is even more accessible than the decision to raise a hand. There is no extra attention or pressure from the decision to engage. This strategy decreases stress and makes quitting less likely. It also increases the value students gain from participation. Answering questions in front of the class is primarily for the benefit of teachers because they learn how well their students understand the content. At best, they may award some participation points. There is little reason, outside of the desire to impress the teacher, for any of the students to cooperate with such little value attached to their action. Pear Deck, however, sends a record of each response a student makes to the student's account, so the answers can serve as a reference for future learning. This tool rewards the teacher and student more equally from class interactions.

Online cloud storage of student work makes their previous learning accessible from any device, any time. This function is the other key to using technology to limit quitting caused by expectations for class participation. If teachers force students to rely on their memories before responding, then those with poor recall or less confidence can't participate as readily. When we ask students to take part in demonstrations of their learning, we try to anchor them in previous assignments. They can use their phones or computers to pull up their resources and use that information to frame their responses. Those who are accustomed to quitting because they have low optimism when it comes to their memory can now work on an equal footing with the rest of the class.

In the scenario at the opening of this section, only three to five students participated, leaving few opportunities for most of the class. The teacher wondered which students understood the subject, which simply chose not to engage, and which remained silent because they didn't understand at all. While answering questions in class may lead to Quit Points, the proper use of technology offers students a better experience, and teachers better feedback on student understanding. It shifted our focus and addressed the reasons why students were reluctant to participate, and changed the way we used digital resources. Using programs that allow students to engage smoothly and without judgment from their peers or teacher will increase opportunities for engagement and reduce quitting.

TAKING OWNERSHIP THROUGH 21ST-CENTURY TOOLS

Today's lesson went remarkably well. Students participated for the entire class, and the work they produced reflected a high level of understanding. They turned their assignments in to the right bin, and the teacher filed them away to later reward the learning in the grade book.

This type of day should inspire celebration. Unfortunately, this system creates problems because the teacher owns all the work, and must organize and store the assignments long enough to assess and catalog individual progress. Students must wait, sometimes for weeks, before they can access their work. This wait for the return of assignments and quizzes can create Quit Points. They hesitate to do new tasks because the teacher didn't return their graded work.

Technology helps solve this problem of ownership by allowing students to access their work anytime. The teacher and student can both view work from any device, simultaneously. This approach means they can use every assignment to support new work. It also takes the stress off students who feel the pressure to submit perfect products. In a traditional paper-and-pencil classroom, teachers treat student work as "final copies." The biggest perfectionists may even refuse to turn in partially complete work if they feel it doesn't meet their standards. Since technology allows students to have access to their assignments at all times, they can modify or revise their work whenever needed. This strategy helps demonstrate that mistakes are a natural part of the learning process—instead of an obstacle that can lead to Quit Points.

The shared nature of digital tools also offers an opportunity to increase the task value of assignments. Blogging, website creation, and other media offer outlets for students to creatively showcase their learning with their peers and community. Broadening the audience beyond the teacher and opening up work for critique or celebration rather than applying a grade, motivates a higher level of engagement. The first time a group of our students shared their work on Padlet, they noticed that they received comments from students from another school. They were proud of the unsolicited praise they received, and when they relayed their experience with the rest of the class, almost everyone asked if they could also publish their work using this tool. An assignment that could otherwise lead to quitting by many students instead resulted in high engagement, because people outside of the school environment became part of the audience.

To make publishing as easy as possible, we allow students to use whatever format works best for them. Our guideline when they are choosing platforms is to decide whether they can access and use the tool in under 60 seconds. The more time that people spend getting comfortable with the technology, the less likely they are to follow through with that resource. As an example, some students feel comfortable designing websites because they have experience in that format. The steps in web design do not hinder them, and they flourish in crafting their finished products. The method includes creativity and design, and results in products that blend multimedia and written examples of learning. Their finished products are worthy of digital publishing. Other students may find the obstacles of web design to be too overwhelming, and prefer to use a different format, such as blogging, for showing their content understanding. The creativity that inspires some students may be a hindrance to others who want to complete assignments in more straightforward ways. Allowing students to choose their optimal experience and exercise their creativity gives them the best opportunity for learning and reduces the obstacles that cause Quit Points.

TEACHER TAKEAWAY

Regardless of what one hears at a tech conference, technology is not the solution to problems in education. And no matter what frustrated teachers post on social media, technology is not the problem, either. It is a tool that helps us avoid moments when students are prone to quitting. Schools should use digital resources and devices because of their value in society, but must keep the student experience in mind or they will give those students more opportunities to quit. When you're considering how to best use technology in the 21st-century classroom, consider student accessibility, value, and overall experience as your determining factors. When technology helps you dodge Quit Points, it unlocks greater student potential for learning.

Collaboration	
Limited	❑ Teachers do not provide opportunities for students to share and collaborate through educational technology ❑ Teachers assume students collaborating through technology to be cheating ❑ Teachers only use paper and pencil resources
Progressing	❑ Teachers use technology for special projects in which students need to work in groups ❑ Teachers use technology for assignment-specific tasks such as peer editing ❑ Teachers use technology for resources that extend beyond textbooks
Advanced	❑ Teachers encourage students to use technology to collaborate on their learning ❑ Teachers encourage students to use technology as a means of sharing, reviewing, and revising their work ❑ Teachers provide opportunities for students to use technology to learn with a wide range of resources and media formats

Figure 7.1: Collaboration Rubric

Participation	
Limited	❑ Teachers do not use technology to provide learning opportunities outside of class time ❑ Teachers do not allow students to refer to past assignments during lessons ❑ Teachers do not provide alternate means for students to demonstrate their learning through technology
Progressing	❑ Teachers use technology to make resources available to students outside of class time ❑ Teachers encourage students to use past assignments as review material for summative assessments ❑ Teachers use technology to increase participation and accountability for the entire class
Advanced	❑ Teachers utilize technology as a means to provide flexible pacing and independent learning opportunities outside of class time ❑ Teachers help students learn to scaffold new learning by using past assignments ❑ Teachers use technology as a means for all students, including those who struggle to engage with peers, to demonstrate learning

Figure 7.2: Participation Rubric

Student Ownership	
Limited	❏ Teachers do not use technology because it encourages cheating and plagiarism ❏ Teachers do not allow students to share their work online
Progressing	❏ Teachers use technology for students to access their work on extended assignments such as research papers or projects ❏ Teachers require students to share their work online in order to increase class collaboration
Advanced	❏ Teachers encourage students to work on assignments outside of class ❏ Teachers offer opportunities for students to publish their work online to engage with peers and their community

Figure 7.3: Student Ownership Rubric

CHAPTER 8

QUIT POINT INTERVENTIONS: WHEN THE GOING GETS TOUGH

Implement targeted interventions to address different quitting behaviors

"People are like bicycles. They can keep their balance only as long as they keep moving."
—ALBERT EINSTEIN

IN THE WORLD of technology, there is a concept known as fault tolerance. As systems become increasingly complex, a failure of even one small component could potentially impact the entire operation. So, engineers design the whole system to remain functional even when a part fails, as a safety net for these complicated structures. When the power goes out in most homes, the residents wait for power to return. In a fault-tolerant building, however, generators kick in to power necessary features of the system. As our systems become more complicated, fault-tolerant design becomes more important.

For most of this book, we have described our fault-tolerant design in the classroom. When teaching a room of 30 pupils, many variables can disrupt the entire system. One person having a bad morning can negatively impact everyone else and prevent learning. By asking what makes students quit, we shift our attention from making the entire class work harder to limiting the adverse effect of one individual on the whole group. Using the Quit Point framework allows us to establish a culture that stresses optimism and task value so that learning is still able to occur, even when some students decide to quit.

> A small increase in effort can be the catalyst that supports productive work for the rest of the lesson. When used correctly, these quick interventions can take students from momentary stagnation to productive learning.

When we make every effort to create a positive culture, it is still impossible to prevent every individual from quitting.

People are also complex systems, so any disruption to normal functioning can lead to a Quit Point. Whether you are an elementary teacher who works with the same group of kids all day, or a high school teacher who works with a new batch of students each period, you are dealing with variables. You cannot limit all disruptions through climate and planning. When the going gets tough, Quit Point interventions help prevent the actions of a few from derailing the entire learning process.

Our intervention program varies, depending on the students' frequency and level of commitment to quitting. If a student rarely shows that he or she has reached a Quit Point, the teacher can apply short-term interventions, either directly or through participation in the student community. However, if problems consistently occur, we use targeted actions that address the obstacles of each student. If quitting behaviors are deeply entrenched, we know that we must get help from people outside of the classroom. Ultimately, it is up to the students to decide to stop quitting. It's our job as teachers to provide the support that will help them make that choice.

FIRST RESPONSE: RAPID QUIT POINT INTERVENTIONS

The effort students dedicate to learning ranges from full engagement to sustained quitting. We designed our first-response interventions to deal with Quit Points while students are near the engaged side of the continuum. The goal is to help them initiate actions that increase the energy they dedicate to learning. A small increase in effort can be the catalyst that supports productive work for the rest of the lesson. When used correctly, these quick interventions can take students from momentary stagnation to productive learning. By using them, we can prevent quitting from becoming more entrenched, or a daily habit.

In our first response, we consciously avoid addressing any of the specific behaviors that signal a student has reached a Quit Point. Drawing attention to unproductive behaviors runs the risk of putting students on the defensive. They might dedicate even more energy to ignoring the learning, or start a power struggle, because they feel the teacher is singling them out for a minor act. If you respond with the assumption that a student is still near the productive end of the continuum, you might avoid these negative reactions. Give a student a slight positive nudge at this point, and it might be enough to help them maintain their engagement.

Many of our interventions serve as unsolicited support. Students who are past a Quit Point are not going to ask for assistance because they are no longer putting any effort toward their assignments. By offering help, rather than traditional redirection, you are giving them a non-confrontational signal that they should be more productive. This support can come from the teacher or peers. We often circulate the room when we see students beginning to show signs of quitting, and offer help with the next question, or ask them to add to a response. Another teacher-based strategy is to feign ignorance and ask students to explain simple parts of their assignment. The goal is to initiate a conversation about the work that will make it easier for them to put their ideas to paper. For example, we may compliment students' answers and ask them to explain how they came to their conclusions, or have them describe what part of the assignment they see as most accessible.

These interventions help students shift their energy toward their learning goals and build optimism. We don't criticize the behaviors that indicate quitting, because doing so increases the pressure—and they are already feeling enough of that. This also shows that the teacher is there to support them, and that we appreciate their efforts. Sometimes we even give them the first part of the answer, to instill confidence. Peer interventions are useful as rapid responses, as well. Not every student feels comfortable with the teacher, especially at the start of the year. Leaning on a peer is often less intimidating than working directly with an adult. This strategy helps them maintain optimism, as it is based on established peer relationships. Another way to use peer networks is to ask students to help someone else. Checking on friends and reviewing their work is often enough to spark an idea and build confidence. When you show trust in all students' abilities to help others, despite occasional quitting, you communicate your confidence in their abilities to succeed.

> To decrease the effects of committed quitting, we often modify assignments. Crossing out questions or eliminating parts of a task can make learning much more approachable for a student who has hit a Quit Point.

These strategies are most successful if they don't feel like interventions, and don't have classroom management or discipline as their motivation. When you ask students to help a friend, it is a non-threatening request and will not increase student frustration. Similarly, offering support to a disengaged student puts the focus on academic behavior, instead of quitting. Since we use these strategies for students who recently hit a Quit Point, we designed them to be as non-disruptive as possible. If they become a distraction to the class, it can create new problems by diverting energy away from the work. When these first-response strategies fall short, it means the students are more committed to their quitting and need more direct interventions.

WHAT TO DO WHEN STUDENTS SHOW A COMMITMENT TO QUITTING

If students seem dedicated to quitting, you must do more than just shift their energy toward productive work. These situations need targeted interventions that specifically address what caused the students to reach a Quit Point. We must decrease the effort they have dedicated toward quitting, so they can focus on learning again. Some of the behaviors that teachers find most frustrating fall into this category, such as students who won't put down their cell phones or continuously talk to friends rather than paying attention. It's easy to focus on the distractions students display, but the root of the problem isn't what they are doing. In fact, putting too much emphasis on the source of the distraction can lead to power struggles and more entrenched quitting. The real issue is that they commit so much of their energy to non-academic behavior. When intervention strategies succeed in disrupting the amount of effort they are applying to quitting, students can refocus their energy toward learning.

It is usually easier for teachers to address quitting that is rooted in academic expectations. Some students may lack the stamina to sustain productive effort for an entire lesson, or may experience energy levels that go up and down, depending on the time of day. Others become overwhelmed by subject-specific tasks like reading or math computations. When these obstacles result in a Quit Point, it becomes difficult for them to maintain their focus. Students often meet traditional attempts to intervene with frustration or apathy, because they require students to put effort into tasks they find unrewarding. Our intervention differs because the goal is to limit the impact of quitting. We encourage any productive activity that moves students closer to engagement.

To decrease the effects of committed quitting, we often modify assignments. Crossing out questions or eliminating parts of a task can make learning much more approachable for a student who has hit a Quit Point. This strategy seems like a good deal from their perspective because they can satisfy our expectations without doing all of the original assignment. The benefit of this strategy is that it can prevent the day from being a total loss, and help the student retain at least a portion of the learning goals. We can always go back to missed learning outcomes on days when there are no obstacles to overcome. It is easier to sustain effort in the absence of Quit Points than when energy shifts to non-academic behaviors. We can use any work students do after interventions as a foundation to help them catch up on more productive days.

Positive peer reinforcement is another useful intervention tool. Offering group rewards when everyone completes their assignment may inspire the most productive students to help those who show signs of quitting. If the students who are quitting value the opinions of their peers, they might become more productive. Committed quitting occurs when students give precedence to personal interests over learning goals. For example, they might prioritize talking about a fight among their friends over practicing vocabulary. Since they value peer interaction, adding social components to learning can help shift the attention back to the assignment. The goal of these strategies is to weaken a student's commitment to quitting by offering a productive option that increases participation in learning.

Obstacles that originate outside of class can be more challenging. Stress from family issues, lack of sleep, or distractions caused by social media are beyond the reach of most educators, and often result in committed quitting. When these behaviors stem from a lack of safety and stability, the key to any intervention is showing empathy. Usually, students are not *trying* to misbehave or fall behind. They just don't have enough energy to devote to school. Listening and showing empathy is a crucial step in demonstrating that school can be a safe place. To address this need, we again use the tool of cutting an assignment down and telling the student that he or she can still have a good day by focusing on learning for at least part of the period. This approach provides the support they desperately need, as well as an opportunity to show some learning. Meanwhile, we avoid jeopardizing relationships by recognizing that these actions are a result of obstacles rather than misbehaviors. This strategy leaves the door open for future learning opportunities.

It's not always easy to differentiate between when students are dealing with severe stressors or when they're just distracted.

The behavior we observe is sometimes identical in both situations. For example, when students refuse to put down a mobile device or to break off a conversation, they might be prioritizing socializing and entertainment over learning, and our primary goal is to disrupt their focus on non-academic actions. It's hard for them to continue their game, conversation, or social media interactions if the teacher sits down to interrupt and ask about their day. Sometimes it's most effective when we don't even address the behavior we're trying to solve. Students who commit to quitting expect us to redirect them and are prepared to rebuff or ignore regular interventions. Inquiring about weekend plans, joining the conversation, or asking them to explain the game they're playing is effective because it breaks their concentration in a friendly manner, and they are unlikely to resist. Once they've shifted their attention away from the distraction, we can suggest that it might be a good time to return to work. Since the commitment to quitting has decreased due to a successful intervention, they will be more likely to refocus on academics than if we told them to put down their phones or stop talking.

This second level of interventions requires more time than first-response strategies because we need to understand why students are committed to quitting. Those strategies work because students don't heavily engage in any activity, so a gentle nudge is enough to prevent quitting and connect them back to their learning goals. However, once students have reached a Quit Point and devoted their energy to staying there, we need to give a targeted response to interrupt that commitment. For most students, showing empathy for their situation or disrupting their quit behavior is enough to redirect them toward learning for at least part of the lesson. Our emphasis on non-confrontational, positive interactions is enough because most students want to succeed and appreciate the opportunities to do so.

Unfortunately, a small portion of students spends most of their time past their Quit Points. They require an even more direct approach that confronts their quitting and disengagement head-on to bring them back into the academic community.

A PLAN TO ADDRESS PERSISTENT QUITTING

Students whose default behavior is quitting are the ones who reach their Quit Points before they even set foot in a classroom. The mere thought of school is enough for them to give up because they have no expectations for academic achievement, or because they struggle with severe long-term obstacles. Most interventions are ineffective when it comes to addressing persistent quitting, since teachers assume that students will try to avoid negative academic and behavioral consequences. This assumption may be valid for most students, but punishment or failure do not deter those who quit by default. Indeed, those are the results they expect. Successful interventions must rely on resources outside the classroom and rehabilitate the students' relationship with the *concept* of school. This requires long-term support and patience while they learn that being a student doesn't always result in overwhelmingly negative experiences.

The most important step when beginning interventions for persistent quitting is to have an honest conversation in which the students acknowledge that they are frustrated in school and aren't showing effort toward learning. If they don't understand that their actions cause problems, they will continue to resist help. Students who are fully committed to quitting have grown used to teachers going out of their way to help them. In fact, teachers usually work much harder than the student in these situations. We encourage the students to take the first step and acknowledge that they need help—and at that point we can start repairing their relationship with school and learning.

We start by asking this group to share their highs and lows to show that we understand that they have bad days—while emphasizing that they have also had good days. Once they define what it means to have a good day, they start to understand how their actions were the determining factors in their success. This awareness helps them find strategies that allow them to take more ownership over their school experiences. Many of these students have poor relationships with teachers due to their own resistance to interventions and lack of participation and achievement. If they don't feel they have personal control over the outcome of their day, they will also feel as if they can't trust the adults around them to care enough to help.

It is this relative lack of good relationships with school personnel that makes it so important to be careful and consistent with support from outside the classroom. Counselors, social workers, administrators, community volunteers, and family members can provide vital assistance to help students in improving their educational experience. As one person, it is easy to feel overwhelmed by the amount of time this process will take, including showing the need for change and then supporting the students as they begin their journeys. Staff members should put together a focused support team to help coordinate the intervention plan, so staff can work more consistently to help students.

The final step of the intervention plan for habitual quitters is to redefine success in school. Once students show the ability to have more positive interactions and achievements, we want them to re-evaluate goals. Their initial understanding of a "good day" was based on overwhelmingly negative experiences. As these become less common, it is easier for them to visualize and plan for even better results in school. At this point, students will articulate goals that include less quitting than before. As their acceptance and commitment to quitting decreases, productive engagement will become their new default behavior.

The intensive nature of this process requires a significant time investment from adults if it is to succeed. This doesn't mean that peers can't be an essential part of the support system. Creating a "buddy system" of mentors provides an additional layer of support.

We establish mentoring relationships that match students who managed to overcome this level of quitting with those who still show minimal engagement in learning. Students who learned to power through their Quit Points are often more realistic role models than teachers who presumably never faced similar struggles.

Understand that disciplinary problems and academic failure will persist during the intervention process, due to the long-term nature of the support plan. Progress and improvement will be evident on some days and seem to disappear on others. As educators, we cannot always react on these students' worst days because our role is as much to ensure the safety of the rest of the class as it is to support the frustrated students. Mentors, however, can serve as advocates and support no matter the situation. We encourage the students who work through this intervention process to text and contact their buddies or mentors when they are most frustrated. This strategy often de-escalates volatile situations and prevents issues that might distract the students from their improvement.

The longer a student accepts persistent quitting, the more difficult it will be to achieve a successful outcome. Teachers need to communicate with colleagues to identify these students as quickly as possible so they can begin the intervention process before quitting is thoroughly entrenched as part of a student's identity. If students give up entirely, it might lead to truancy, in which case it will become even more difficult to reach them. We need all students to come to school to build on their positive experiences so they have enough optimism to persevere through tough times. Working with a network of educators and peer mentors helps build relationships that can motivate even the most troubled students to go to school. If they attend, there are always opportunities to create the positive experiences and reflection necessary to lead even the most persistent of quitters back to productivity.

TEACHER TAKEAWAY

Most Quit Point strategies use preventive measures to avoid and limit quitting. However, everyone reaches Quit Points from time to time, no matter how much we try to avoid them. When teachers recognize disengagement, they might use one of three levels of intervention, all geared toward varying degrees of quitting. The first level of rapid response interventions are designed to be quick, non-threatening, and used with all students. If students are merely distracted but not devoting energy toward another activity, these strategies can quickly shift their focus toward productive learning. Even when they don't succeed, these interactions might diagnose more severe problems.

If students have committed to quitting, second-level interventions focus on breaking the attention they have devoted to non-academic behaviors by initiating manageable productive actions. Finally, those students who struggle with habitual quitting need intensive mediation that goes beyond traditional classroom interventions. Teachers can use the interventions to create environments that maintain relationships with these students, increase positive learning experiences, and keep the door open for future interactions.

First Response Interventions	
Limited	❑ Teachers publicly correct behavior with directives
	❑ Teachers respond emotionally to behavior issues
	❑ Teachers take sole responsibility for all behavior management
Progressing	❑ Teachers try to minimize disruption to class when correcting behavior
	❑ Teachers maintain calm when addressing student behavior
	❑ Teachers highlight positive role models to the class
Advanced	❑ Teachers use behavior concerns as an opportunity for relationship building
	❑ Teachers maintain a positive, supportive attitude when addressing behavior
	❑ Teachers facilitate support from peers in order to prevent behavior issues

Figure 8.1: First Response Interventions Rubric

Targeted Interventions	
Limited	❑ Teachers get caught in power struggles with students who don't respond to initial interventions
	❑ Teachers successfully stop undesirable behavior but do not re-engage students in learning
	❑ Teachers emphasize personal control over the classroom climate
Progressing	❑ Teachers understand that some disengagement is caused by stressors instead of poor behavior
	❑ Teachers successfully shift some of the attention to learning but students maintain a below-average level of engagement
	❑ Teachers work to include students when establishing a classroom climate
Advanced	❑ Teachers provide support to students based on the reason they are disengaged
	❑ Teachers intervene and successfully return the focus to academics
	❑ Teachers facilitate a classroom climate in which peers initiate support to disengaged students

Figure 8.2: Targeted Interventions Rubric

Long-Term Interventions	
Limited	❑ Teachers stop attempting interventions for students who are not disruptive when disengaged ❑ Teachers do not try to enlist the support of staff and family when providing interventions ❑ Teachers expect interventions to work quickly and do not allow enough time to see results
Progressing	❑ Teachers consistently provide opportunities for students to participate even if they normally disengage ❑ Teachers work with colleagues to learn new strategies for interventions ❑ Teachers expect successful interventions to transition to other classes and grades
Advanced	❑ Teachers commit to attempting a variety of interventions until they see a positive impact ❑ Teachers work as a team with other educators and community members to ensure sufficient support is in place ❑ Teachers facilitate interventions for extended periods (including from year to year) to ensure student improvement is maintained as they transition to new grades

Figure 8.3: Long-Term Interventions Rubric

CHAPTER 9

CASE STUDIES: HOW QUIT POINT IMPACTS REAL STUDENTS

See examples of student achievements through the successful use of Quit Point strategies

"The ability to move others hinges less on problem solving than on problem finding."
—DANIEL PINK IN *TO SELL IS HUMAN*

WE WERE EXCITED to see positive effects for many of our students when we began implementing our framework for dealing with students who quit. There was less quitting, more effort, and increased engagement in the learning process. Several students showed improvement that was beyond all our expectations. They either overcame more considerable obstacles than we thought possible or achieved results greater than anything we'd seen in the past. This section showcases several individuals of various skill levels to demonstrate the possible achievements from our program. We both had years of experience in a traditional system before changing our approach due to our Quit Point research. Not once in the past did any student accomplish the dramatic improvement we've learned to anticipate under our new framework. While not every student will reach the level of achievement in these examples, we witnessed a transformational impact that boosted the effort of the entire class.

Names have been changed to protect student anonymity.

MARISHA

Marisha entered her freshman year full of confidence and with aspirations of studying medicine in college. She was friendly and responsible, and expected the transition to high school to be a smooth one. Unfortunately, things didn't go as well as she hoped. There was much more emphasis on reading and writing than in previous years, and she quickly fell behind in her history and English classes. Since she was always playing catch-up, it was hard for her to show sufficient learning to earn the type of grades expected of future doctors. Marisha avoided any support or interventions because she was afraid of negative feedback from her teachers. Her avoidance became so entrenched that she eventually stopped participating in classes at all. Suddenly, repeating her freshman year seemed like a more realistic possibility than college. A meeting with Marisha, her parents, and the grade-level administrator became the catalyst we needed to turn things around. Maybe she wasn't the excellent student she thought she was. Perhaps she was even better.

In the meeting, we found that the root of Marisha's problems was that her self-perception didn't match her achievement. She was reluctant to dedicate more effort toward learning because she felt that her effort went unrewarded. Instead of telling her to try harder, we changed the focus to her behavior after quitting. Since she tried to withdraw due to frustration, we decided to emphasize participation. The class game offered an easy way to scaffold her engagement into more academic work. All she had to do was complete the introductory challenge and use her rewards to gain power. Within a week, Marisha had earned the ability to take leadership over a third of the class. This leadership provided her with the positive reinforcement and achievement she desperately needed. Her peers looked to her as an example of how to succeed, and she gained confidence as her experiences changed from negative to positive.

In fact, she loved being a leader so much that she continued to increase her power. During the unit on World War I, we provided rules that teams could use to conquer other groups. Marisha soon became the leader of a 40-person empire spread out over three class periods. She created government systems to reinforce her rule, and a hierarchy of students reported their achievements on team challenges to their leader.

This success also translated into academics. Marisha benefited from the feedback and support we provided as she integrated into the class culture. Her work improved, and she started showing mastery on every learning target. Since she was the first layer of support for her empire, she also refined her learning through interactions with and assistance to her peers. She took this responsibility seriously, because helping people was of important personal value. The reason she was interested in medicine was because she wanted to help people. The role of leader allowed her to do just that.

She began asking her business teacher for permission to do her work before school, so she would have time during fifth period to help teammates in other classes. She was able to make enough time during her lunch and her business class to interact with all the students that she conquered. They were expected to share their work with her so she could give support if needed. She would either message them on the document or come in for a short visit whenever she recognized that anyone on her team was struggling. Marisha also reinforced our daily action goals, such as improving an answer or supporting a peer, to help everyone focus on growth. In the end, it wasn't just Marisha who saw her achievement improve. Her entire team demonstrated more learning and success under her leadership.

Most impressive of all was that her strategies were entirely her idea. She taught us more about how class leaders could work than we ever expected. It turns out she was right in the first place. Marisha eventually smoothly transitioned to high school once she addressed her Quit Point problem. She continued to demonstrate leadership in clubs and extracurricular activities and used the cooperative learning skills she mastered in our class to graduate with honors. She is now in college and working toward her goal of a career in medicine.

DRAKE

Drake wasn't supposed to accomplish much in high school. The school district identified him as one of the freshmen least likely to earn enough credits to become a sophomore. After he failed to meet any of the requirements for his core classes in middle school, the district socially promoted him to high school. Drake came into our class seeing himself as a "dumb kid" and talking about dropping out as soon as he turned 16. He hated to sit at a desk like the rest of his peers, and when he did finally sit down, it was usually to take a nap. He would lay on the counter in the back of the room or walk around the classroom to start each day. His peers were frustrated by our expectation that they try to be inclusive and collaborate with Drake. They assumed he wouldn't contribute—and were almost always right.

Drake only socialized with other students who were similarly disengaged, so he didn't trust any peers who would be able to provide support. We hoped that the class game would be enough to change his mindset about learning, by demonstrating that our approach wasn't quite like what he expected. Unfortunately, we were wrong. He either refused to participate or wanted to lose and return to quitting as quickly as possible. Nonetheless, we kept encouraging inclusiveness from other teams, and tried to help Drake build positive experiences. Students continued to express dismay at the thought of having to work with someone who wouldn't contribute to the group. Eventually, it was their complaints that became the catalyst for a dramatic turnaround.

The team leaders decided to start a lottery in which students could buy-in with their reserves of awarded classroom currency to win all the money in the jackpot. Drake had developed an antipathy toward the rest of the class based on their constant complaining about him, and decided he wanted to continue to disrupt the other teams. If he could manage to win the lottery, he could influence the game so that the kids who

> Things changed at that moment, because Drake realized that he did care about something. ... Our primary goal for the game was to facilitate engagement in class, so it was easy to accommodate this role of a saboteur in our rules.

disliked him would be disappointed. His friends pooled all their class currency and then bought 80 lottery tickets for Drake. The plan worked. Drake won the lottery and a large sum of class money. For the first time all year, he was happy because the rest of the class couldn't believe he, of all people, was the winner. The game had always motivated these students and they put so much energy into winning, yet by sheer luck and 80 lottery tickets, Drake had won—and he didn't even care.

Since both groups were so interested in the results of the game, we used this opportunity to encourage friendly competition and better integrate all students into the class.

Things changed at that moment, because Drake realized that he did care about something. He liked making all his peers who looked down on him lose in the class game. Our primary goal for the game was to facilitate engagement in class, so it was easy to accommodate this role of a saboteur in our rules. Instead of using teacher-created obstacles to challenge teams as they competed, we created a way for Drake to be the obstacle. The self-named "Slacker Team" appointed him as their king and worked to gain enough power to outperform everyone else. To accomplish this goal, Drake, as the leader, had to fulfill new responsibilities. If his team didn't show productivity during class, they would not be allowed to sabotage and obstruct.

Drake developed better work habits and became a mentor for his peers. He would regularly remind his team that if he could do it, anyone could. Then they would move into a circle and make sure they completed all assignments. For the first time, the entire class took part in the learning process, and five students who had previously never earned a passing grade started demonstrating proficiency and comprehension. What began as sabotage became the structure needed to support multiple persistent quitters. By the end of the year, Drake learned to be confident in his ability to succeed in the classroom. He also learned that he could win the game. Most important, this positive experience transformed his opinion of school, as he continued to show growth and learning in the following years.

CASSIE

Cassie's maturity was evident from the moment she stepped foot in the classroom. She was conscientious about schoolwork and kind to all her peers. In many ways, she was precisely the type of student that teachers hope to find on their rosters. She participated faithfully in team challenges, enjoyed the class game, and thoughtfully responded to feedback on assignments. It didn't take long for Cassie to show consistently high levels of achievement and earn the respect of her peers for her reliable contributions to team success. All this suggested she would have a smooth and productive year in our class. Then one day it got complicated.

Cassie's team was consistently among the highest performers. At this point, we had two high schools that simultaneously participated and competed in our class game. We used a scoreboard to track the achievements of every team, and her team was always near the top. This success ran into an unexpected obstacle. Her team leader was absent for multiple days and didn't interact with anyone while away from school. It was his responsibility to organize strategies to complete challenges and plan for the success of the team. Other leaders communicated via text or social media whenever they were away from school, but Cassie's leader seemed to go off the grid. When he finally returned to class several days later, he ignored and laughed off his team's concerns about his ability to fulfill the responsibilities he'd accepted as the leader.

During this time, our game focused on modeling the problems and ideas from the Industrial Revolution. Cassie came to us asking if there was a way she could replace the leader with someone more responsible. We informed her that, based on the rules of the game, she needed to find a way to remove him that aligned with what we were studying. Cassie returned the next day after a night of independent study and informed us that she was going to start a socialist revolution modeled after the ideas of the early workers' movement. She spoke to her team and encouraged them to unite to remove their irresponsible leader, who was absent again that day, so that they could work together for a better future. Her words inspired her team, and when the leader came back to class, they went on strike and successfully convinced him to resign.

Cassie was proclaimed the new leader by her admiring team, but she didn't want to reproduce the system they had used under their previous leader. She tried to fulfill the promises of her revolution, declaring that they would operate under democratic principles from that point forward, and that they would all share in the wealth (based on class currency) that they earned as a team. The revolution was a success, and her team reached new levels of productivity due to their engagement with the system she created. This achievement carried over to their academic responsibilities. They used their inclusive democratic process to work together and provide support to all members. Some days, when the team had consensus that they didn't perform as well as they hoped, they voted to assign themselves homework so they could catch up before the next class. As one of the most influential students, Cassie oversaw everyone's learning and made sure no one fell behind.

Everything worked so well after the revolution that Cassie decided she needed to share their success with all the teams in both schools. She wanted everyone to be as happy as her group was now that they worked together and shared all benefits and responsibilities. Cassie wrote an email to relay her story to all the students in both schools, hoping it would help them take control over their teams and benefit all members.

She attached some of the posters and slogans that inspired her team, with the assumption that it would have a similar effect on everyone else. This noble gesture didn't go as she had hoped. The students in the other school were suspicious and assumed her messages were a trick designed to undermine their teams. Leaders demanded that all members of their groups delete any emails from outside groups or risk expulsion for disloyalty. As each side communicated their suspicions to the other, a sense of identity similar to nationalism developed at each school. They were proud of their teams and wanted to protect themselves from potentially dangerous outside influences. This pride resulted in incredible motivation to succeed in both the team game and academics. Leaders started class each day with speeches about the importance of learning and academic effort so that they could show the other school that they were able to match any achievement.

What started as a revolution to protect the interests of her peers became a friendly competition between students in both schools to show their abilities and strengths. This competition was like a shot of adrenaline that led most students to dedicate more energy to learning than they had ever done in the past. Cassie didn't only lead her team to a better future; she led the freshmen classes of two schools to better achievement than ever before. We learned as much as any of our students. It was incredible how much impact the actions of one individual could make on the lives of hundreds of people. It was also exciting to see that our class game could facilitate collaboration between school districts. Cassie finished the year amazed at the impact her kindness and goodwill had on others. Even though not everyone responded as she had hoped, her ability to make a difference encouraged her. Cassie continued to dedicate herself to supporting others and became active in helping those in need in her community. She always knew she was a good person; now it was also clear that she could change the world.

THE REALITY IS THAT EVERYONE QUITS. NOT ONLY IS IT HUMAN NATURE, BUT IT'S ALSO A LOGICAL AND PREDICTABLE BEHAVIOR UNDER THE RIGHT CONDITIONS.

CONCLUSION

A FINAL DOSE OF
TEACHER OPTIMISM

"Let us remember: One book, one pen, one child, and one teacher can change the world."
—MALALA YOUSAFZAI

NE DAY, AS we were discussing plans for our next lesson, one of our highest-achieving students stopped by to talk. She was distraught because several of her teachers had discouraged her from pursuing her dream job. Ever since she was little, her goal was to be a teacher because she wanted to help people. As a high-achieving student who loved learning, she believed she would be qualified to work in our profession. When she shared her plans, these teachers told her teaching was a terrible job. They told her that teachers don't receive respect from students or politicians, and spend so much time worrying about data, valued-added measures, and meetings that they can't do their jobs. We tried to provide encouragement. Certainly, teaching can feel like a thankless job, and these frustrations can be overwhelming at stressful times, but it can be a great career and a tremendous opportunity to make a difference. We assured this student that if she wanted to work in education, it was her choice to make.

She walked out feeling a little better, but still conflicted about her future. Instead of imagining a career in which she could help and inspire people, she now worried that one day, she too would be so unhappy that she would caution students away from teaching. This conversation made us reflect on the start of our journey of discovery. Frustration was also an

> We had to stop thinking of each student as a hard worker or a slacker and recognize the complexity and unique nature of individuals' strengths and obstacles.

important part of our story. We decided to experiment with new tools and strategies because we were frustrated at how difficult it was to make an impact on some students. There were days when we felt like we wasted all the effort we put into our lessons because too many students went home without learning. Sometimes we spent more energy correcting behavior than we did teaching.

That frustration continued even after we incorporated the latest tools and strategies from educational research. Too many students still showed too little progress. No wonder so many teachers are resistant to professional development. Every book, conference, and strategy has the potential to transform and improve the classroom, but it can be hard to focus on the improvement when a few students continue to resist any attempt at learning. Even videos of highly engaged students working in other schools can have a demoralizing effect if teachers don't think they will ever see similar results in *their* classes. When this type of frustration takes control of their thinking, it's easier to make an excuse for sticking to the status quo than it is to try something new. Teachers blame the tools or the students to justify why they can't improve their teaching.

What saved us from this cycle of frustration was the realization that we were missing an essential part of the teaching process. We had to stop thinking of each student as a hard worker or a slacker and recognize the complexity and unique nature of individuals' strengths and obstacles. There was no universal method or strategy a teacher could implement to cure the problems of education. However, there was a question that nobody seemed to be asking. Understanding what makes students quit was our eureka moment. Recognizing Quit Points helped us uncover the impact of student effort on learning.

We had previously assumed that every student who was cooperative was also trying, and students who were resistant were slacking off. Like most teachers, we didn't try to measure effort. We used variables like grades, politeness, and even body posture to make rough approximations that frequently told us more about compliance than they did about academic engagement. No wonder we were disappointed by the results of our instruction. We were too busy looking for body posture to recognize when students were learning. Instead of focusing on how much effort students put into their work, we worried about whether their assignments were complete. Quit Point helped us realize that what we assumed to be effective classroom monitoring had distracted us from more useful information.

After we focused on preventing Quit Points, many teaching strategies that previously seemed cumbersome or ineffective became a regular part of our practice. We finally understood why so many administrators and teachers called ideas like differentiation, collaboration, and teaching with technology "best practices." It wasn't that we were using the wrong tools; we hadn't considered the role that student effort had on the success of the learning process. The energy students give to learning can range from high engagement to a complete shutdown. We couldn't just expect our instructional strategies to improve effort. We had to plan lessons that limited the obstacles to participation, and established a classroom climate that taught students how to be more resilient in the face of challenges.

We had spent our entire professional careers under the

assumption that the actions of teachers were the driving force in student success. Plug in the right strategy and voila—learning happens. We had been conditioned to accept that our effort was the variable that made it all possible. Just like Ptolemy, the ancient astronomer, toiling to justify the scientific inaccuracies of a geocentric universe, teachers had been struggling to solve the inadequacies of our educational system. No amount of math in the world could displace the sun from the center of the universe, and no amount of teacher effort could perfect learning. Educators need a new truth, a new framework, which uses the understanding of student effort to begin reshaping what children can accomplish in and outside the classroom.

Once we shifted our focus to Quit Points, it opened up a new world. There were so many nuances to the level of effort students gave to learning—and we were starting to recognize them as more than just whether students were trying or not. We also began to see the limits of traditional motivational strategies, which relied too heavily on students sharing the values of their teachers. One of the most difficult lessons was that effort didn't always look the way we expected. Often, students weren't working hard because they realized they could succeed with a fraction of their maximum effort. Sometimes students who regularly checked text messages and talked with friends were more productive than peers who quietly maintained focus on their assignments. This understanding helped us recognize quitting and disengagement more quickly, which improved the efficiency of our interventions.

The most unexpected benefit of our Quit Point framework

was how it helped us better collaborate with colleagues. Previously, we focused our discussions on pacing and project ideas within our department, but when solving Quit Points is your focus, you don't need to stay on a similar schedule or even teach the same subject to work together with other teachers. We started working with a team of teachers from multiple school districts and various subject areas to share ideas about how to maximize student effort and avoid Quit Points. Sometimes the best insights for a math class came from a social studies teacher. At other times, suburban teachers learned how to improve gifted education from colleagues in a large urban district. Quit Point offered a universal vocabulary and filter that allowed us all to work together, regardless of our teaching styles or levels of experience.

The reality is that everyone quits. Not only is it human nature, but it's also a logical and predictable behavior under the right conditions. Even when teachers do everything in their power to prevent quitting, there are times when unexpected reactions and responses will require quick interventions. As much as adults like to focus on persevering, we quit more than we'd like to admit, and kids are no different. The G.I. Joe cartoon taught us that "knowing is half the battle," and recognizing that students are complicated people with a tendency to quit when the going gets tough is the first step to making school a place that empowers them rather than allows them to fail. Whether Quit Points occur from an unpredictable emotional reaction, or from a decision to save energy for other priorities, our response to quitting will play a large part in determining the strength of our relationships with students.

Just like parents are there to support their children, whether they are at their best or throwing a tantrum, teachers need to ensure that students feel supported regardless of whether they give effort or quit.

Sometimes the best strategies to limit quitting require creative thinking. Even the most organized lesson plans and engaging projects won't be enough to maintain every student's engagement. Just like all adults know they are supposed to save for retirement and have regular check-ups with a doctor and dentist, but find reasons not to, students will experience situations that prevent responsible decisions. When it comes to our health and financial stability, we accept the fact that some people need a nudge to make the best choices. Teachers also need to learn to experiment and find what will push our students to maintain engagement. We didn't plan to help our students build nation-states or make our class website look like a smartphone screen. Those were adjustments based on what we observed from students, and the feedback we received when we asked students to reflect on their Quit Points.

Whether it's through building optimism and task value, establishing resilient behaviors, or lessening the impact of obstacles, the role of the teacher has changed. Adopting a mindset based on understanding Quit Points and their effect on effort is the new job of educators. We are no longer a sage on the stage, but instead we are facilitators of empowerment. How we adapt to our new role will determine what is possible in learning. Borrowing again from Sir Arthur C. Clarke, we are confident that the future of education "will be fantastic." We've had a glimpse of that future over the past four years, and we're now more enthusiastic about teaching than ever before. We leave school every day with a better understanding of the success of our lessons, and we know what to do if things don't go as planned. Gone are the days when we drove home frustrated and exhausted. We can proudly say that teaching is a fantastic job, and it feels great to make a difference.

APPENDIX A

A QUIT POINT TEACHER'S TOOLKIT

BLENDED TIER ASSIGNMENT TEMPLATE

We designed this template to help teachers differentiate assignments to assess students of varying skill levels who are working on identical projects. The Level 1 prompts evaluate a student's progress toward understanding and comprehending the content standards (in line with Bloom's taxonomy). The Level 2 prompts focus on skills of application and analysis of the content. The Level 3 prompts provide opportunities for students to synthesize and evaluate their learning and to take more ownership. While assessing student responses, the teachers should not try to find right and wrong answers. Instead, they should identify the area most in need of feedback and improvement. If a student is getting stuck on knowledge-level content questions, the second- and third-level questions are not relevant to providing focused feedback. Likewise, if a student has already demonstrated strong understanding and skills related to a content standard, there is no need to devote attention to those questions. The teacher can assess backward, starting with the Level 3 questions.

Directions:

- Keep as simple and streamlined as possible.
  - ➤ Example: "Answer the prompts using your reading."

Questions:

- **Level 1 prompt targeting knowledge:** Ask students to recall, remember, define, match, describe, select, etc.

- Example: "Describe what happened when more force was applied to the wagon.")

- Example: "Define isosceles."

- Example: "What is the inverse operation of addition?"

- **Level 1 prompt targeting comprehension:** Ask students to explain, estimate, compare, summarize, etc.

  - Example: "Summarize the main idea of the story."

  - Example: "Compare the characteristics of an isosceles triangle to the characteristics of an acute triangle."

  - Example: "Compare the different strategies to solve the problem, aka long vs. synthetic division, or factoring vs. quadratic formula."

- **Level 2 prompt targeting application:** Ask students to solve, relate, interpret, etc.

  - Example: "Relate the outcome of the story to current events."

  - Example: "Cite three different combinations of coins needed to purchase a $0.50 snack."

  - Example: "Solve the equation. What does your result mean, in context?"

- **Level 2 prompt targeting analysis:** Ask students to classify, categorize, conclude, etc.

- ► Example: "Classify the following arguments into Federalist or Anti-Federalist views."

- ► Example: "Explain the mathematical strategy used to solve the equation, and provide steps in the process."

- **Level 3 prompt targeting evaluation:** Ask students to evaluate, appraise, support, defend, etc.

  - ► Example: "Evaluate the effectiveness of the speaker's argument."

  - ► Example: "Decide which estimate is closest to the correct solution."

  - ► Example: "What was the student doing correctly, when solving incorrectly?"

- **Level 3 prompt targeting synthesis:** Ask students to create, hypothesize, invent, adapt, rewrite, etc.

  - ► Example: "Rewrite three events from Hamlet to drastically impact the end of the play."

  - ► Example: "Create a triggered device that can accurately launch a ping-pong ball at targets of specified distances."

  - ► Example: "When you are simplifying square roots, you look for pairs. What would you do with cube roots? What would be the same or different?"

TIER 1 ASSIGNMENT TEMPLATE

This template is designed to help teachers modify assignments for students who are struggling to demonstrate an understanding of content standards and basic skills. The resources used should be at or just above skill level, to prevent Quit Points. Resources that connect to prior knowledge can also provide scaffolding support to help students through the lesson. Prompts should focus primarily on knowledge and comprehension of content. Once students are showing steady effort and understanding at this level, they should move up to Tier 2 assignments that focus on skills and higher-level learning.

Directions:

- Keep as simple and streamlined as possible.

  - Example: "Answer the prompts using your reading."

Questions:

- **Level 1 prompt targeting knowledge:** Ask students to recall, remember, define, match, describe, select, etc.

  - Example: "Describe what happened when more force was applied to the wagon."

  - Example: "Define isosceles."

  - Example: "What is the inverse operation of addition?"

- **Level 1 prompt targeting comprehension:** Ask students to explain, estimate, compare, summarize, etc.

- ► Example: "Summarize the main idea of the story."

- ► Example: "Compare the characteristics of an isosceles triangle to those of an acute triangle."

- ► Example: "Compare the different strategies to solve the problem, aka long vs. synthetic division, or factoring vs. quadratic formula."

Extension Question:

- **Level 2 prompt targeting application:** Ask students to solve, relate, interpret, etc.

  - ► Example: "Relate the outcome of the story to current events."

  - ► Example: "Cite three different combinations of coins needed to purchase a $0.50 snack."

  - ► Example: "Solve the equation. What does your result mean, in context?"

TIER 2 ASSIGNMENT TEMPLATE

This template is designed to help teachers modify assignments for students who have shown understanding of content standards and basic skills, but need to focus attention on refining mid-level skills of application and analysis. The resources used should be at or just above skill level to prevent Quit Points. Once students are showing steady effort and understanding on this level, they should move up to Tier 3 assignments that focus on depth of knowledge and critical thinking skills.

Directions:

- Keep as simple and streamlined as possible.

  - Example: "Answer the prompts using your reading."

Questions:

- **Level 1 prompt targeting comprehension:** Ask students to explain, estimate, compare, summarize, etc.

  - Example: "Summarize the main idea of the story."

  - Example: Compare the characteristics of an isosceles triangle to the characteristics of an acute triangle."

  - Example: "Compare the different strategies to solve the problem, aka long vs. synthetic division, or factoring vs. quadratic formula."

- **Level 2 prompt targeting application:** Ask students to solve, relate, interpret, etc.

  - ► Example: "Relate the outcome of the story to current events."

  - ► Example: "Cite three different combinations of coins needed to purchase a $0.50 snack."

  - ► Example: "Solve the equation. What does your result mean, in context?"

- **Level 2 prompt targeting analysis:** Ask students to classify, categorize, conclude, etc.

  - ► Example: "Classify the following arguments into Federalist or Anti-Federalist views."

  - ► Example: "Explain the mathematical strategy used to solve the equation, and provide steps in the process."

Extension Question:

- **Level 3 prompt targeting evaluation:** Ask students to evaluate, appraise, support, defend, etc.)

  - ► Example: "Evaluate the effectiveness of the speaker's argument."

  - ► Example: "Evaluate which estimate is closest to the correct solution."

  - ► Example: "What was the student doing correctly, when solving incorrectly?"

TIER 3 ASSIGNMENT TEMPLATE

This template is designed to help teachers modify assignments for students who have shown an advanced understanding of content standards and skills. The resource should be challenging, to stretch the learning of the students. Questions should focus primarily on evaluation and synthesis. An extension question provides an opportunity to move on to future learning or demonstrate significantly advanced skills. The goal for Tier 3 assignments is not to penalize these students with more work, but to offer a similar amount of work that provides a more significant challenge.

Directions:

- Keep as simple and streamlined as possible.

    ► Example: "Answer the prompts using your reading."

Questions:

- **Level 2 prompt targeting analysis:** Ask students to classify, categorize, conclude, etc.

    ► Example: "Classify the following arguments into Federalist or Anti-Federalist views."

    ► Example: "Explain the mathematical strategy used to solve the equation, and provide steps in the process."

- **Level 3 prompt targeting evaluation:** Ask students to evaluate, appraise, support, defend, etc.

- ➤ Example: "Evaluate the effectiveness of the speaker's argument."

- ➤ Example: "Evaluate which estimate is closest to the correct solution."

- ➤ Example: "What was the student doing correctly, when solving incorrectly?"

- **Level 3 prompt targeting synthesis:** Ask students to create, hypothesize, invent, adapt, rewrite, etc.

  - ➤ Example: "Rewrite three events from Hamlet that would drastically impact the end of the play."

  - ➤ Example: "Create a triggered device that can accurately launch a ping-pong ball at targets of specified distances."

  - ➤ Example: "When you are simplifying square roots, you look for pairs. What would you do with cube roots? What would be the same or different?"

Extension Question:

- Opportunity to look ahead at future learning or skills: Ask students to predict, reflect, or learn an advanced skill.

BLUEPRINT TEMPLATE

Having a single common target for all students to reach can potentially cause Quit Points if they do not see the possibility of success or value in the assignments. This template provides questions to consider for students approaching proficiency, at proficiency, or at mastery of the standard, to better account for those needs. Begin the process by identifying the specific learning outcome. Then use the questions to consider how each level of student will demonstrate understanding of the standard, what assessment will be used to measure that understanding, and the skills necessary to the process.

Learning standard to teach:

Approaching Proficiency (Tier 1):

- What will the student show to demonstrate mastery of the standard?

- What is the assessment used to measure mastery?

- What skills will be the focus of assignments?

Proficient (Tier 2):

- What will the student show to demonstrate mastery of the standard?

- What is the assessment used to measure mastery?

- What skills will be the focus of assignments?

Mastery (Tier 3):

- What will the student show to demonstrate mastery of the standard?

- What is the assessment used to measure mastery?

- What skills will be the focus of assignments?

LESSON PLAN TEMPLATE

While many daily lesson plans focus on learning objectives and procedures, we use our blueprinting process to organize those elements. Our daily lessons focus on building optimism, providing focused feedback, and offering students opportunities to explore and extend their learning. Use the following template to build your own lesson plans and organize them for the best student learning and engagement.

Lesson Plan	
Optimism	❏ Provide an opportunity to start the lesson with optimism. This can connect to previous learning, allow for collaboration with peers, or focus on competing in a game or challenge.
Feedback	❏ Provide an assignment that students can work on individually or with their peers ❏ Assess student progress during this time and provide focused feedback for improvement
Exploration and Extension	❏ Provide opportunities for students to explore and extend their learning once they have met the goals for the lesson

Figure A.1: Lesson Plan

ACTION GOALS TEMPLATE

Students can use these checklists to self-monitor their academic behaviors throughout the lesson. Instead of you using them as class rules, put your students in charge of managing these actions. The first-step actions are designed to prepare students for learning and ensure that they do not fall into quitting behaviors.

The second-step actions are designed to guide students through productive academic behaviors during the lesson. The goal is not to merely complete the assignment, but to challenge oneself. This stage is where the bulk of the learning occurs for most students.

The third-step actions are designed to provide higher-level academic behaviors that not all students will necessarily reach. They set the tone that high-level learning does not take place only through completion of work. Self-reflection and responding to focused feedback are how students develop long-lasting improvement. These are general templates designed to reduce Quit Points, but you can modify them to fit the specific needs of each classroom.

Team Members		
1st Step Actions	❏ (a specific student action to show they've started the lesson) ❏ (a specific student action to show they've reduced distractions to learning) ❏ (a specific student action to aid in initiating the lesson) ❏ (ex - I've attempted the first question)	
2nd Step Actions	❏ (a specific student action to show they're progressing through the lesson) ❏ (a specific student action to show they have sought out additional help or feedback) ❏ (a specific student action to show they are collaborating) ❏ (a specific student action to extend student learning) ❏ (ex - I've improved an answer on my own) ❏ (ex - I've thought about how this assignment connects to other learning)	
3rd Step Actions	❏ (a specific student action to show they are nearing the end of the lesson) ❏ (a specific student action to show they have sought out feedback from the teacher) ❏ (a specific student action to extend learning after feedback) ❏ (a specific student action to show they collaborated with peers) ❏ (ex - I've checked in with the teacher) ❏ (ex - I've improved an answer based on teacher feedback)	

Figure A.2: Daily Action Goals for Team Members

Team Leaders		
1st Step Actions	❑ (a specific leader action to show leadership and collaboration with their team) ❑ (ex - My teammates have started their assignment) ❑ (ex - My teammates are making progress on their assignment)	
2nd Step Actions	❑ (a specific leader action to verify group progress) ❑ (a specific leader action to show collaboration) ❑ (ex - I've checked in with the teacher to report group progress) ❑ (ex - I've helped a teammate)	
3rd Step Actions	❑ (a specific leader action to verify group success) ❑ (ex - I've communicated the group's achievements with the teacher) ❑ (ex - I've checked to ensure the group understands the lesson)	

Figure A.3: Daily Action Goals for Team Leaders

FEEDBACK TEMPLATE

This checklist is designed to help you quickly assess student work and provide focused feedback on improving it. When students are struggling to meet learning standards, it means they need continued practice in the lower levels of Bloom's taxonomy (knowledge and comprehension). Providing specific feedback and opportunities to help them focus their efforts on activities that are designed to reinforce their learning will help to close any gaps relative to their peers. Rather than offering more information, give these students content-specific examples, main ideas, and vocabulary that strengthen their understanding of the standard. Once students have shown a proficient level of knowledge, focus on skills of application and analysis. Emphasize comparisons, supporting evidence, collaboration, and organization to help strengthen the skills necessary to move to deeper levels of learning.

Once students show mastery of the content and skills, they need opportunities to evaluate and synthesize their understanding. Asking students to analyze, make connections, and reflect upon their learning will offer structure to extend well beyond the standard.

Feedback	
Content	❑ Student is not yet proficient or showing basic proficiency ❑ Student should focus on vocabulary, main ideas, and providing examples
Skills	❑ Student shows moderate proficiency and is focused on communicating a range of learning ❑ Student should focus on comparisons, supporting evidence, collaboration, and organization
Depth	❑ Student begins to demonstrate mastery of the material at an advanced level ❑ Student should focus on analytical thinking, making connections to personal life, reflection, and complexity

Figure A.4: Feedback Model

SAMPLE GAME

As stated in the book, we created a game that runs through the entire school year. The goal is to blend content with the collaborative culture of the classroom. Below are the details for the game we used during the unit on the Industrial Revolution. It is important to keep in mind that this is not a simulation designed to result in a predetermined outcome. Once the rules are established, it is up to the students to think creatively, work collaboratively, and have fun taking control of the learning process.

Student Roles:

- Team leaders become capitalist factory owners.

- Team members become the assembly line workforce.

- The team leader may hire one team member to manage the assembly line work for the rest of the team.

Payments:

- Factory owners are paid based on the number of trains the team produces within the challenge time.

- Factory owners can use their daily payment to pay workers as they see fit.

- Factory owners will be able to invest extra capital in stock shares of other class companies.

Rules:

- Workers can be fired if they are preventing the group from achieving its best work. Fired workers must move to the "unemployment" table, from which another team can hire them.

- Factory owners cannot be fired.

- Each team member is only allowed to produce two parts of the train. 'Copy and Paste' is not allowed unless the 'Die Casting Cheat Code' is purchased by the factory owner.

Cheat Codes:

- $30 Mechanization Cheat Code: Allows team members to complete more than two steps each.

- $30 Die Casting Cheat Code: Allows team members to copy and paste individual parts of the train.

Stock Market:

- Stock prices are determined by meeting daily quotas.

- Prices will go up or down based on the team's ability to meet quota each week.

- Factory owners who own stock in another company can cash out their stocks at any time, at market value.

Products:
- Google Drawing TRAIN assembly line

- ► Step 1: Create and name the drawing (Product 1, Product 2, Product 3, etc.), then share with the person next to you.

- ► Step 2: Create the first rear wheel and then share it with the person next to you.

- ► Step 3: Create the second rear wheel and then share it with the person next to you.

- ► Step 4: Create the front wheel and then share it with the person next to you.

- ► Step 5: Create the main body and then share it with the person next to you.

- ► Step 6: Create the chimney and then share it with the person next to you.

- ► Step 7: Create the conductor's cabin and then share it with the person next to you.

- ► Step 8: Create the smoke out of the chimney and share it with the manager.

- ► Repeat your step over and over and over until your manager lets you stop.

step 1: Create and Name

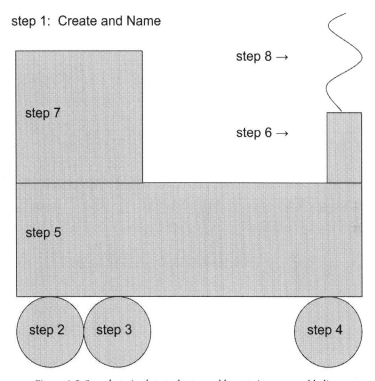

Figure A.5: Sample train that students would create in an assembly line.

SAMPLE SOCIAL STUDIES ASSIGNMENT

This assignment addresses subject-specific content, while also allowing students of various skill levels to address the topic at multiple degrees of depth. Initial questions are designed to measure knowledge and comprehension, while additional questions ask students application- and analysis-level questions. The group discussion and collaboration on answers allows students of all skill levels to participate and learn from their peers. The writing prompt at the end of the lesson asks students to summarize and demonstrate their understanding of the subject.

1. The class uses a reading on the Scientific Revolution. After each section, students discuss in groups a question related to the notes, and collaborate on an answer. Repeat this process through each section of the reading.

    a. How might people have tried to prove something was true before the scientific method? Which groups in society would have the most say over what was true?

    b. How did the telescope make the solar system seem less "heavenly"? What was actually viewed through the telescope?

    c. Newton used science to prove things existed that couldn't be seen or touched. If people are capable of such amazing achievements, how might people start looking at human nature differently?

d. How did scientific discoveries prove that people could be important to their country in ways outside of the organization of Feudal society?

2. At the end of the section questions, each student will write his or her own summary regarding the topic.

   a. In a paragraph, summarize the main idea of the Scientific Revolution. Think about answering this question using the ideas of what, when, who, how, and why, to set up your response.

      i. What (What is it, in your own words?)

      ii. When (When did these new ideas take place?)

      iii. Who (Who are the most important figures we need to know and what did they do?)

      iv. How (How did these new ideas come out? How did they change life?)

      v. Why (Why is this important?)

SAMPLE COLLABORATIVE SOCIAL STUDIES ASSIGNMENT WITH TECHNOLOGY

This assignment uses technology to allow students to collaborate on a single assignment, while using different resources that express varying points of view and emphasis.

1. Students work in groups of three on the same Google Doc. Each student has a different resource and set of questions to answer.

   a. Student 1:

      i. What are two reasons the United States entered WWI?

      ii. Was this good or bad for Germany? Why?

      iii. Why was the United States able to help win the war?

   b. Student 2:

      i. What are two reasons Russia was unsuccessful in WWI?

      ii. Was this good or bad for Germany? Why?

      iii. Why couldn't Russia handle total war?

   c. Student 3:

      i. Why did Germany surrender?

      ii. Why did Germany think the peace treaty was unfair?

  iii. Which countries had the biggest losses in WWI?

2. Once each student has completed the reading and questions, each member of the group discusses his or her topic and answers to the questions.

3. After all three students have had an opportunity to share their specific topics, each student answers an open-ended writing prompt individually. All three answers can be seen on the document, allowing for peer review.

  a. Use total war to explain why some countries had to give up fighting during WWI.

  b. Explain why the United States was so important, even though it didn't fight very much.

  c. Explain why Germany was so upset by the Treaty of Versailles.

COMPARING TIER 2 AND TIER 3 MATH ASSIGNMENTS

The Tier 2 assignment uses more explicit instruction and is broken into steps for the students. Breaking the question into steps provides support in solving the problem, while also giving the teacher feedback about where any deficiencies may occur in the process. Question 5 provides another opportunity if the student struggles on the previous questions.

Tier 2 Math Assignment

1. What variable is not used in the continuously compounded interest formula, that is used in the compound interest formula?

2. What new number is used in the continuously compounded interest formula?

3. You had a summer job, and at the end of the summer you had earned $1,500. You then decided to invest your money in a savings account that earned 5 percent annual interest, compounded continuously.

    a. Identify P, r, and t.

    b. Write an equation to find out how much money will be in the account after three years.

    c. How much money will be in the account after three years?

4. Say you want to deposit $30 into a savings account to save money to buy birthday presents for your family.

The account earns 7 percent annual interest, compounded continuously.

    a. Identify P, r, and t.

    b. Write an equation to find out how much money will be in the account after one year.

    c. How much money will be in the account after two years?

5. Additional practice: You want to buy a building in three years that you can make into your own restaurant. To save money, you deposit $400 into a savings account that earns 4 percent annual interest, compounded monthly.

    a. Identify P, r, and t.

    b. Write an equation to find out how much money will be in the account after three years.

    c. How much will be in the account after three years?

The Tier 3 assignment is less structured than the Tier 2 assignment, because students have already demonstrated understanding of the procedures. There is no need to break the problem down into steps or provide supports.

Tier 3 Assignment

1. What equation will you use if an account is compounded continuously?

2. What equation will you use if an account is compounded annually?

3. An investment of $13,000 is made into a checking account by the local fire department in order to save money to build a new fire station. If the account earns 6 percent annual interest, how much will be in the account if it is compounded:

    a. Semi-annually for three years?

    b. Continuously for three years?

4. When you were born, your parents put $15,300 into a savings account, to save money in case you decided to go to college. The account earned 3 percent annual interest. How much will be in the account after 18 years if it is compounded:

    a. Annually?

    b. Continuously?

HACKING EDUCATION
10 Quick Fixes For Every School

By Mark Barnes (@markbarnes19) & Jennifer Gonzalez (@cultofpedagogy)

In the award-winning first Hack Learning Series book, *Hacking Education*, Mark Barnes and Jennifer Gonzalez employ decades of teaching experience and hundreds of discussions with education thought leaders to show you how to find and hone the quick fixes that every school and classroom need. Using a Hacker's mentality, they provide **one Aha moment after another** with 10 Quick Fixes For Every School—solutions to everyday problems and teaching methods that any teacher or administrator can implement immediately.

"Barnes and Gonzalez don't just solve problems; they turn teachers into hackers—a transformation that is right on time."

—Don Wettrick, Author of *Pure Genius*

HACKING PROJECT BASED LEARNING
10 Easy Steps to PBL and Inquiry in the Classroom
By Ross Cooper (@rosscoops31) and Erin Murphy (@murphysmusings5)

As questions and mysteries around PBL and inquiry continue to swirl, experienced classroom teachers and school administrators Ross Cooper and Erin Murphy have written a book that will empower those intimidated by PBL to cry, "I can do this!" while at the same time providing added value for those who are already familiar with the process. Impacting teachers and leaders around the world, *Hacking Project Based Learning* demystifies what PBL is all about with **10 hacks that construct a simple path** that educators and students can easily follow to achieve success. Forget your prior struggles with project based learning. This book makes PBL an amazing gift you can give all students tomorrow!

"*Hacking Project Based Learning* is a classroom essential. Its ten simple 'hacks' will guide you through the process of setting up a learning environment in which students will thrive from start to finish."

—DANIEL H. PINK, *NEW YORK TIMES* BESTSELLING AUTHOR OF *DRIVE*

HACKING ASSESSMENT
10 Ways To Go Gradeless In a Traditional Grades School

By Starr Sackstein (@mssackstein)

In the bestselling *Hacking Assessment,* award-winning teacher and world-renowned formative assessment expert Starr Sackstein unravels one of education's oldest mysteries: How to assess learning without grades—even in a school that uses numbers, letters, GPAs, and report cards. While many educators can only muse about the possibility of a world without grades, teachers like Sackstein are **reimagining education**. In this unique, eagerly-anticipated book, Sackstein shows you exactly how to create a remarkable no-grades classroom like hers, a vibrant place where students grow, share, thrive, and become independent learners who never ask, "What's this worth?"

"The beauty of the book is that it is not an empty argument against grades—but rather filled with valuable alternatives that are practical and will help to refocus the classroom on what matters most."

—Adam Bellow, White House Presidential Innovation Fellow

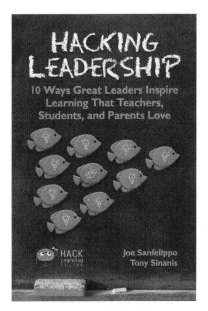

HACKING LEADERSHIP
10 Ways Great Leaders Inspire Learning That Teachers, Students, and Parents Love

By Joe Sanfelippo (@joe_sanfelippo) and Tony Sinanis (@tonysinanis)

In the runaway bestseller *Hacking Leadership*, internationally known school leaders Joe Sanfelippo and Tony Sinanis bring readers inside schools that few stakeholders have ever seen—places where students not only come first but have a unique voice in teaching and learning. Sanfelippo and Sinanis ignore the bureaucracy that stifles many leaders, focusing instead on building a culture of **engagement, transparency and, most important, fun**. *Hacking Leadership* has superintendents, principals, and teacher leaders around the world employing strategies they never before believed possible and learning how to lead from the middle. Want to revolutionize teaching and learning at your school or district? *Hacking Leadership* is your blueprint. Read it today, energize teachers and learners tomorrow!

"The authors do a beautiful job of helping leaders focus inward, instead of outward. This is an essential read for leaders who are, or want to lead, learner-centered schools."

—GEORGE COUROS, AUTHOR OF *THE INNOVATOR'S MINDSET*

HACKING SCHOOL CULTURE
Designing Compassionate Classrooms

By Angela Stockman (@angelastockman) and Ellen Feig Gray (@ellenfeiggray)

Bullying prevention and character-building programs are deepening our awareness of how today's kids struggle and how we might help, but many agree: They aren't enough to create school cultures where students and staff flourish. This inspired Angela Stockman and Ellen Feig Gray to begin seeking out systems and educators who were getting things right. Their experiences taught them that the real game changers are using a human-centered approach. Inspired by other design thinkers, many teachers are creating learning environments where seeking a greater understanding of themselves and others is the highest standard. They're also realizing that compassion is best cultivated in the classroom, not the boardroom or the auditorium. It's here that we learn how to pull one another close. It's here that we begin to negotiate the distances between us, too.

"*Hacking School Culture: Designing Compassionate Classrooms* is a valuable addition to the Hack Learning Series. It provides concrete support and suggestions for teachers to improve their interactions with their students at the same time they enrich their own professional experiences. Although primarily aimed at K–12 classrooms, the authors' insightful suggestions have given me, a veteran college professor, new insights into positive classroom dynamics which I have already begun to incorporate into my classes."

—LOUISE HAINLINE, PH.D., PROFESSOR OF PSYCHOLOGY, BROOKLYN COLLEGE OF CUNY

HACKING EARLY LEARNING
10 Building Blocks to Success in Pre-K–3 That All Teachers and School Leaders Should Know

By Jessica Cabeen (@jessicacabeen)

School readiness, closing achievement gaps, partnering with families, and innovative learning are just a few of the reasons the early learning years are the most critical years in a child's life. In what ways have schools lost the critical components of early learning—preschool through third grade—and how can we intentionally bring those ideas and instructional strategies back? In *Hacking Early Learning*, kindergarten school leader, early childhood education specialist, and Minnesota State Principal of the Year Jessica Cabeen provides strategies for teachers, principals, and district administrators for best practices in preschool through third grade, including connecting these strategies to all grade levels.

"Jessica Cabeen is not afraid to say she's learned from her mistakes and misconceptions. But it is those mistakes and misconceptions that qualify her to write this book, with its wonderfully user-friendly format. For each problem specified, there is a hack and actionable advice presented as "What You Can Do Tomorrow" and "A Blueprint for Full Implementation." Jessica's leadership is informed by both head and heart and, because of that, her wisdom will be of value to those who wish to teach and lead in the early childhood field."

—RAE PICA, EARLY CHILDHOOD EDUCATION KEYNOTE SPEAKER AND AUTHOR OF *WHAT IF EVERYBODY UNDERSTOOD CHILD DEVELOPMENT?*

HACKING ENGAGEMENT
50 Tips & Tools to Engage Teachers and Learners Daily

By James Alan Sturtevant (@jamessturtevant)

Some students hate your class. Others are just bored. Many are too nice, or too afraid, to say anything about it. Don't let it bother you; it happens to the best of us. But now, it's **time to engage!** In *Hacking Engagement*, the seventh book in the *Hack Learning Series*, veteran high school teacher, author, and popular podcaster James Sturtevant provides 50—that's right five-oh—tips and tools that will engage even the most reluctant learners daily. Sold in dozens of countries around the world, *Hacking Engagement* has become an educator's go-to guide for better student engagement in all grades and subjects. In fact, this book is so popular, Sturtevant penned a follow-up, *Hacking Engagement Again*, which brings 50 more powerful strategies. Find both at HackLearningBooks.com.

HACKING DIGITAL LEARNING STRATEGIES
10 Ways to Launch EdTech Missions in Your Classroom
By Shelly Sanchez Terrell
(@ShellTerrell)

In this breakthrough book, international EdTech presenter and NAPW Woman of the Year Shelly Sanchez Terrell demonstrates the power of EdTech Missions—lessons and projects that inspire learners to use web tools and social media to innovate, research, collaborate, problem-solve, campaign, crowd fund, crowdsource, and publish. The 10 Missions in *Hacking DLS* are more than enough to transform how teachers integrate technology, but there's also much more here. Included in the book is a **38-page Mission Toolkit**, complete with reproducible mission cards, badges, polls, and other handouts that you can copy and distribute to students immediately.

"The secret to Shelly's success as an education collaborator on a global scale is that she shares information most revered by all educators, information that is original, relevant, and vetted, combining technology with proven education methodology in the classroom. This book provides relevance to a 21st-century educator."

—THOMAS WHITBY, AUTHOR, PODCASTER, BLOGGER, CONSULTANT, CO-FOUNDER OF #EDCHAT

HACKING CLASSROOM MANAGEMENT
10 Ideas To Help You Become the Type of Teacher They Make Movies About

By Mike Roberts (@baldroberts)

Utah English Teacher of the Year and sought-after speaker Mike Roberts brings you 10 quick and easy classroom management hacks that will make your classroom the place to be for all your students. He shows you how to create an amazing learning environment that actually makes discipline, rules, and consequences obsolete, no matter if you're a new teacher or a 30-year veteran teacher.

"Mike writes from experience; he's learned, sometimes the hard way, what works and what doesn't, and he shares those lessons in this fine little book. The book is loaded with specific, easy-to-apply suggestions that will help any teacher create and maintain a classroom where students treat one another with respect, and where they learn."
—CHRIS CROWE, ENGLISH PROFESSOR AT BYU, PAST PRESIDENT OF ALAN, AUTHOR OF *DEATH COMING UP THE HILL, GETTING AWAY WITH MURDER: THE TRUE STORY OF THE EMMETT TILL CASE; MISSISSIPPI TRIAL, 1955*

HACKING THE WRITING WORKSHOP
Redesign with Making in Mind
By Angela Stockman (@AngelaStockman)

Agility matters. This is what Angela Stockman learned when she left the classroom over a decade ago to begin supporting young writers and their teachers in schools. What she learned transformed her practice and led to the publication of her primer on this topic: *Make Writing: 5 Teaching Strategies that Turn Writer's Workshop Into a Maker Space*. Now, Angela is back with more stories from the road and plenty of new thinking to share. In *Make Writing*, Stockman upended the traditional writing workshop by combining it with the popular ideas that drive the maker space. Now, she is expanding her concepts and strategies and breaking new ground in *Hacking the Writing Workshop*.

"Good writing is good thinking. This is a book about how to think better, for yourself and with others."

—DAVE GRAY, FOUNDER OF XPLANE, AND AUTHOR OF *THE CONNECTED COMPANY*, *GAMESTORMING*, AND *LIMINAL THINKING*

The uN series

THE UNSERIES Teaching Reimagined

The uNseries is for teachers who love the uNlovable, accept the uNacceptable, rebuild the broken, and help the genius soar. Through each book in the uNseries, you will learn how to continue your growth as a teacher, leader, and influencer. The goal is that together we can become better than we ever could be alone. Each chapter uNveils an important principle to ponder, uNravels a plan that you can put into place to make an even greater impact, and uNleashes an action step for you to take to be a better educator. Learn more about the **uNseries and everything uN** at unseries.com.

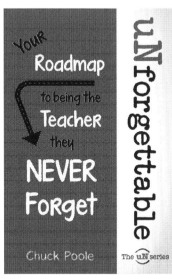

uNforgettable
Your Roadmap to Being the Teacher They Never Forget
by Chuck Poole (@cpoole27)

"These 10 destinations will give you the inspiration and knowledge you need to take action and leave a lasting impression for years to come. Chuck Poole will be your guide. Through every twist and turn, you will be empowered, encouraged, and equipped to reimagine teaching in a way that will influence your students for a lifetime."

RESOURCES FROM TIMES 10

SITES:
times10books.com
hacklearning.org
hacklearningbooks.com
unseriesbooks.com
teachonomy.com

PODCASTS:
hacklearningpodcast.com
jamesalansturtevant.com/podcast
teachonomy.com/podcast

FREE TOOLKIT FOR TEACHERS:
hacklearningtoolkit.com

ON TWITTER:

@HackMyLearning
#HackLearning
#HackLearningDaily
#WeTeachuN
#HackingLeadership
#HackingMath
#HackingLiteracy
#HackingEngagement
#HackingHomework

#HackingPBL
#MakeWriting
#EdTechMissions
#MovieTeacher
#HackingEarlyLearning
#CompassionateClassrooms
#HackGoogleEdu
#ParentMantras
#QuitPoint

HACK LEARNING ON FACEBOOK:
facebook.com/hacklearningseries

HACK LEARNING ON INSTAGRAM:
hackmylearning

ABOUT THE AUTHORS

Adam Chamberlin earned a B.A. in Communication from Cleveland State University and a M.Ed. from Ohio State University. He has worked in both private and public sectors of education, and currently teaches high school social studies at Franklin Heights High School in Columbus, Ohio. He continues to serve on leadership committees at the building and district levels, and is a national presenter at professional education conferences. Adam is the co-founder of Pomme LLC, an educational consulting firm. He lives in central Ohio with his wife and two sons.

Sveti Matejic earned his B.A. and M.Ed. from Ohio State University. He continues to teach history at Franklin Heights High School in Columbus, Ohio, where he began his career in 2004. He is a recipient of the Teacher of the Year award and District Ambassador Award for his frequent presentations at professional conferences. He is also a department chair and member of the district curriculum committee. Sveti also pursues his interest in teaching and working with young people through coaching. He has 16 years of experience in youth soccer, and currently coaches with Ohio Premier. Sveti is the co-founder of Pomme LLC, an educational consulting firm. He lives in central Ohio with his wife, son and daughter.

ACKNOWLEDGMENTS

JOINT ACKNOWLEDGMENTS

WE WOULD LIKE to thank a handful of people who had an immense impact on our professional journey, and our work on Quit Point. Several district-level administrators believed in our initial ideas enough to provide encouragement. Thank you to Margaret Towery and Erik Shuey: Your support created the momentum that led to a revolutionary change in how we taught. Without that help, we could still be spinning our wheels. A special thanks to Tom Reed, who was the first person to recognize the potential impact of Quit Point. We are extremely grateful for his guidance throughout this process. We would not be where we are without his mentoring and guidance. We would also like to thank our publisher, Mark Barnes at Times 10 Books. It's exciting to think a few messages on Twitter led to sharing our ideas with a whole new audience. We appreciate the support through this daunting process of publishing. A very special thanks to our friend and colleague, Alex Blohm, who provided the math examples found in this book. We never would have guessed that a collaboration between social studies and math teachers would change how both subjects are taught. Finally, a colossal thanks to our families, who supported us in every imaginable way throughout this process.

ADAM'S ACKNOWLEDGMENTS

First and foremost, I need to thank my wife and sons for the sacrifices they made that allowed me to work on this project. Whether it was giving up evenings or weekends, or simply being supportive as the deadline approached, I could not have made it through without your amazing support. Parenting helped to make me a better teacher, and the ideas in this book continue to make me a better parent. With that being said, I also want to thank my parents for the example they set. They modeled hard work and perseverance, and always stressed doing my best. I was constantly reminded of their parenting style through the writing of this book. They were my first teachers, and I can't thank them enough for all that they've done. Finally, I want to thank my friend and co-author for embarking on this immensely difficult task. Who knew how hard it would be to write a book? At least we went through it together.

SVETI'S ACKNOWLEDGMENTS

I would like to thank my family for the enthusiasm they've shown for every part of this project. My wife, as a fellow educator, actively supports the development of all the ideas that are part of our Quit Point framework. She is a partner in everything I do, and this was no exception. My children helped make this an enjoyable experience through the attentiveness and playful energy that they infused into our home. My parents and brother are the primary reasons why I never settle for conventional wisdom or simple solutions. Their high standards and appreciation of travel, culture, and reading prepared me to always search for new experiences and opportunities. Their example helped give me the confidence to explore and pursue all my dreams. This pursuit led me to meeting so many supportive people, whether through travel, teaching, or coaching, who always had time for a word of encouragement. Finally, to Adam: I couldn't ask for a better friend or collaborator. I don't know how far we would have gone without being able to tackle this project as a team.

PUBLICATIONS

Times 10 is helping all education stakeholders improve every aspect of teaching and learning. We are committed to solving big problems with simple ideas. We bring you content from experts, shared through multiple channels, including books, podcasts, and an array of social networks. Our mantra is simple: Read it today; fix it tomorrow. Stay in touch with us at Times10Books.com, at #HackLearning on Twitter, and on the Hack Learning Facebook page.

Made in United States
Orlando, FL
23 September 2022

22693704R00146